The Comprehensive High School

BOOKS BY JAMES B. CONANT

The Comprehensive High School

Shaping Educational Policy

The American High School Today

The Child, the Parent, and the State

Education in the Junior High School Years

Slums and Suburbs

The Education of American Teachers

The
Comprehensive
High School

a second report to interested citizens by

James B. Conant

Chairman of a Committee of the National Association
of Secondary School Principals on a Study
of the American Secondary School

McGraw-Hill Book Company · New York · Toronto · London · Sydney

Acknowledgments

1401031

The National Association of Secondary School Principals has generously financed this study. Carnegie Corporation of New York has made possible my participation. In the summer of 1965 the Executive Secretary and President of the National Association of Secondary School Principals proposed that the Association finance a study which I might conduct and which would be of interest to the Association. After a short discussion it was agreed that the study should be in the nature of a second look at the American High School. It soon developed that the only practical way of carrying out an inquiry on a national basis would be by means of questionnaires. Therefore, a committee was organized to formulate the necessary documents and review the returns. The committee was composed as follows: James B. Conant, Chairman; Nathaniel Ober, Vice Chairman; George E. Shattuck, Associate Director; Robert L. Foose, Samuel M. Graves, Warren C. Seyfert, Ellsworth Tompkins, Eugene Youngert, and Douglas W. Hunt as a Special Consultant. I undertook the responsibility of writing the reports with the understanding that the members would not be responsible for any of the statements;

neither, of course, would the National Association itself. Nevertheless, I believe that the conclusions have the full approval of the members of the committee.

It should be clear to anyone who has undertaken this type of study that the success depends on the collective wisdom of all involved. In this case the Associate Director, Mr. George E. Shattuck, who devoted full time to the undertaking, was indispensable. He has been, in fact, the director of the entire enterprise. In collaboration with Mr. Hunt and Dr. Seyfert of the Washington office of the National Association of Secondary School Principals, he supervised the sending out of the questionnaires and the processing of the data.

As Chairman of the committee and the author of this report, I take this opportunity to acknowledge our indebtedness to all the members of the National Association of Secondary School Principals who have cooperated with us in the enterprise. Any one who finds our report of interest and value should thank the principals who have cooperated by promptly filling out and returning the questionnaires.

James B. Conant

National Association of Secondary School Principals
1201—16th Street, N.W., Washington, D.C. 20036,
November 1, 1966

Contents

CHAPTER ONE

The Comprehensive High School: An American Invention

In 1957 I started a study of the American comprehensive high school. The results were published in 1959 in a little book entitled *The American High School Today: A First Report to Interested Citizens.* The present volume is a second report. It is concerned primarily with the opportunities for studying a variety of subjects in 2,000 widely comprehensive schools of medium size. Although I have revisited recently a number of the schools I examined in 1957, I have done so mainly to renew my acquaintance with those who are dealing daily with the problems of a public high school. I have made little attempt in this report to incorporate any conclusions from these visits. What follows is based on written replies to a questionnaire. The limitations of such a procedure are obvious. Many of the most significant characteristics of a high school—in particular the quality of the teaching—remain unassessed. However, while I have been unable to examine many matters of first importance, the coverage of the present inquiry is nationwide; what follows presents the answers to questions addressed to the principals of one category of

1

public high schools in the fifty states. The returns emphasize the great differences among schools and the variations from state to state. If one accepts the criteria set forth in my first report, then one must conclude that only a few of the schools about which we obtained information can be regarded as highly satisfactory. On the other hand, the evidence indicates that the situation regarding academic studies in a great many schools is better than it was ten years ago. The ambition of the community and the money available appear to be the limiting factors.

I am prepared to maintain that an excellent comprehensive high school can be developed in any school district provided the high school enrolls at least 750 students and sufficient funds are available. Inadequate finances spell an unsatisfactory school. Such a conclusion stands out clearly from the present inquiry. As one examines the returns from different schools and different states, it becomes apparent that the American ideal of equality of educational opportunity is far from being realized. What emerges is a challenge to each community and each state. It is quite clear that there is something wrong with the way we finance our public schools. A new look at an old problem is required by state legislatures and the Congress of the United States. It is my hope that the facts presented in the following pages may serve to arouse the informed electorate as to the need for both study and action.

WHAT IS A COMPREHENSIVE HIGH SCHOOL?

The concept of a comprehensive high school is foreign to educators in other countries. It is far from clear to the many Americans who have had no direct contact with our public high schools. Rather than attempt a one-line definition, I shall quote from the Foreword to my first report written by John Gardner, President of the Carnegie Corporation of New York. He wrote as follows:

The comprehensive high school is a peculiarly American phenomenon. It is called comprehensive because it offers, under one administration and under one roof (or series of roofs), secondary education for almost all the high school age children of one town or neighborhood. It is responsible for educating the boy who will be an atomic scientist and the girl who will marry at eighteen; the prospective captain of a ship and the future captain of industry. It is responsible for educating the bright and the not so bright children with different vocational and professional ambitions and with various motivations. It is responsible, in sum, for providing good and appropriate education, both academic and vocational, for all young people within a democratic environment which the American people believe serves the principles they cherish.

The comprehensive school is a product of our history. Each community under authority delegated by the state government was expected to provide free schools. As the high schools developed more than fifty years ago, it gradually became accepted doctrine that instruction should be provided for youth with a variety of ambitions and abilities. In only a few cities did the European idea of separate selective academic high schools take root. Rather, an *elective* system as contrasted to a *selective* system became characteristic of American schools. The high school student was expected to choose a course of study from among a variety of offerings; only a small fraction of time was devoted to required subjects. With the great increase in the numbers attending high school, caused in part by compulsory attendance laws, came an increase in the heterogeneity of the student body. This heterogeneity was recognized early as one advantage of the public high school; boys and girls from different environments came to know one another. Increasing efforts have been made in the last thirty or forty years to insure that by one method or another youth from a variety of backgrounds would come to understand each other. One might almost say that the justification of the American system as contrasted with the European must be in terms of social and political ideals. The comprehensive high school attempts to accomplish these ends: it endeavors to provide a general education for all future citizens on the basis of a common democratic understanding; and it seeks to provide in its elective offerings excellent instruction in academic fields and rewarding first-class vocational education. These tasks are not easy to accomplish. The difficulties have been emphasized time and time again. Yet in spite of all criticism the comprehensive high school remains characteristic today of American public secondary education.

The schools in some of the large cities are an exception to the statement I have just made. Clearly, if some of the public school students in a given district or sub-district attend either a separate academic or a separate vocational school, one cannot say that all those wishing to enroll in a public high school are in one school. Separate academic high schools are rare. At present they exist only in New York City and two or three other localities. Separate vocational schools, however, are to be found in a number of large city districts and as area schools in some states. To the extent that they enroll youth who might otherwise attend the local public high school, their existence limits a statement as to the generality of the comprehensive concept. Actually, for reasons given later, we have included but a handful of high schools in the big cities in the present report. Therefore, the category of schools under consideration may be said to include only comprehensive schools. The nature of the student body of comprehensive schools, however, varies greatly from district to district. This would be true even if all the families sent their children to the public schools, which is far from being the case in some communities. One measure of the differences school by school is the percentage of the graduates proceeding with formal education. Such a measure of heterogeneity I consider profoundly significant because it tells one a great deal about the incomes and aspirations of the families served by a high school. Therefore we have sought to classify all the nation's public high schools according to the percentage of the graduating class which went on for further education. We believe that the 18,500 schools to which we sent a questionnaire include all the public high schools with a 12th grade. We obtained returns from just over 15,000 schools, or 80 per cent. One may conclude that the picture which the results present is a fairly accurate national index of the comprehensiveness of our schools.

The figures showing the distribution of *schools* according to the percentage of the class of 1965 going on with education are given below. They are divided into six categories.

Distribution of schools in terms of the percentage of 1965 graduates who continue full-time education

	Percentage of graduates continuing					
	0–9	10–24	25–39	40–59	60–74	75 and over
Percentage of schools	4.0	13.3	25.6	33.5	16.6	7.0

The reader will note that only about 4 per cent of all the schools have as few as 0–9 per cent of the graduating class going on to further education. At the other end of the scale, only 7 per cent of the schools have 75 per cent and more going on to further education. These figures support the general conclusion that the typical high school of the United States serves a widely heterogeneous student population—heterogeneous with respect to the ambitions of the graduates for further education. It will be noted that over three-quarters of all the responding schools fall in the categories of those from which between 25 per cent and 75 per cent of the graduating class enroll in institutions of higher education. *These schools with a heterogeneous student body*

I have chosen to call widely comprehensive high schools.

Returns from the questionnaire sent to the 18,500 schools also provided information about the organization and size of the schools measured by their total enrollment. Tables I and II in the Appendix summarize the data. Table II lists the number and percentage of schools *in each state* in the following enrollment categories: 0–499, 500–749, 750–999, 1,000–1,999, 2,000 and over. On a national basis the figures are as follows:

	Enrollment				
	0–499	*500–749*	*750–999*	*1,000–1,999*	*over 2,000*
No. of schools	6,763	2,706	1,624	2,863	908
Per cent	45.5	18.2	11.0	19.3	6.1

A glance at Appendix Table II shows the vast variation state by state. For example, while 45 per cent of the 15,069 schools reporting are small schools (that is, with enrollments less than 500), in some states as many as 80 per cent or more high schools are in this category; in other states as few as 15 to 20 per cent, and in one state only 5.2 per cent enroll fewer than 500. What is perhaps most surprising is the small number of large schools (enrollment over 2,000). On a national basis only 908 such schools (or 6.1 per cent of the total) reported.

We do not have accurate figures for the enrollments in the five different groups, nor do we have figures for the percentage pursuing education beyond the high school. We have made rough estimates, however, and conclude that something like a half of all the public high school students in the nation attend schools with an enrollment between 750 and 1,999; about a third are in the small schools (enrollment less than 500) and about 15 to 20 per cent in schools with 2,000 or more students.

As I have already noted, the prime advantage of a comprehensive school over a selective school is the opportunity provided students from different backgrounds to learn how to get on with one another. *If this ideal had been overriding in all states and all communities a century ago, there would have been no segregated schools.* In my first report I made no reference to separate Negro schools. But in a supplementary study, *Slums and Suburbs,* I had much to say about the shocking conditions in the Negro slums of the large cities. Today the situation is changing fast. Because of the rapidity of the change and the difficulty of using a questionnaire to determine the social and economic backgrounds of the students, we decided not to attempt to describe the heterogeneity of the schools except in terms of the further education of the graduates.

DEFINITION OF THE CATEGORY OF COMPREHENSIVE SCHOOLS TO WHICH A SECOND QUESTIONNAIRE WAS SENT

After examining the data provided by the original 15,000 schools which answered the questionnaire sent to 18,500 schools, we decided to concentrate our attention on schools of *medium size*—that is, with a total enrollment of 750–1,999. (Since many schools are three-year schools and others four-year schools, our enrollment criteria are not precise; the figure may refer to either a three-year or four-year school.) We wanted our schools to be typically comprehensive, and therefore we eliminated schools from which less than 25 per cent go on to further education and those from which more than 75 per cent of the graduates proceed with further formal education. From the figures already given, it will be noted that the two groups of schools we did *not* include constitute only some 24 per cent of the public high schools with a 12th grade. We estimated that there were, as of October 1965, about 3,000 schools in the category we had defined; we further estimated that well over one-third of all the public high school *students* in the United States were enrolled in the schools in our classification. Because of incomplete returns and failure to obtain a 100 per cent return, the actual number of schools reporting was just over 2,000. In 1965 these 2,000 schools, with a combined enrollment of almost 2,500,000 students, graduated 641,203 young men and women.

Our definition of the schools on which we wished to focus attention reflects my long-standing interest in the comprehensive high school. The reasons are evident for excluding from this inquiry schools that sent very few on to further education (less than 25 per cent) or from which a large number entered college. Schools in each of these other categories have their own special problems. These schools represent extremes—extremes in social, economic, and racial characteristics of the communities served. I venture to remind the reader that these are the extremes I referred to in *Slums and Sub-*

urbs. As I noted at that time, one type of community had within it social dynamite that would explode with devastating effect unless radical measures were taken. My predictions have proved, unfortunately, all too close to the mark.

We are well aware that the restrictions we placed on size and on the homogeneity of the student body have resulted in eliminating many schools in both rural and metropolitan areas. We have ruled out a number of small schools in rural communities and large high schools in city districts. Our restrictions on percentage going on for further education have eliminated a number of high schools in large cities serving economically depressed and disadvantaged neighborhoods, as well as a number of high schools in the suburbs serving prosperous districts. Thus the schools on which I am reporting in the present volume include, for example, only one school in Chicago, two in St. Louis, one in Philadelphia, three in New York City, four in Detroit, two in Los Angeles, and one in San Francisco. The chief reason for ruling out schools with an enrollment of over 2,000 was the realization that most of these exist within our large cities. As I have stressed so often in the past, many of these schools present special problems. For instance, I still believe that schools in disadvantaged communities should have a far larger staff than would normally be necessary. This need has been recognized in some cities, and steps to improve the situation are now being taken.

To sum up, the category of public high schools to which we sent a second questionnaire and on which I am reporting is defined as including only widely comprehensive schools as measured by the percentage of graduates in 1965 who pursued a formal education (25 per cent to 75 per cent). It is further defined as comprising schools of medium size (enrollment between 750 and 2,000). The distribution according to size of the schools in this group that reported is given in the following table.

TABLE 1.   Number and percentage of the 2,024 medium-size comprehensive high schools reporting,
distributed among three categories according to size

Size measured by enrollment	Schools reporting		Enrollment October 1, 1965		Graduates 1965	
	No.	%	No.	%	No.	%
750–999	681	33.6	590,412	23.8	147,031	22.9
1,000–1,499	841	41.5	1,026,033	41.3	266,800	41.6
1,500–1,999	502	24.8	863,921	34.8	227,372	35.4
TOTAL	2,024		2,480,366		641,203	

Let me anticipate at this point some of the data to be presented in the following chapters by recording that, contrary to my expectations, the size of the school within the limits we set is an important but not a determining factor when a comparison of the adequacy of the course offerings is made. Far from it. Whether a school has an enrollment of 750 or 2,000 (the limits of our category), size seems to make little difference except in two respects: the school's ability to offer a wide program in foreign language, and its ability to offer students opportunities for advanced placement. These depend to some extent on the size of the school.

As might have been predicted, the number of schools with three or more assistant principals is greater when the enrollment is between 1,500 and 1,999 than when the school is smaller.

If the size of the school within our limits is not the determining factor in regard to many of the measurable qualities of the school, one may well ask what is. Is there any pattern to the significant differences among schools? An attempt to answer this question leads at once to an exploration of inequalities of educational opportunity, as evidenced by our inventory of the course offerings and practices in 2,000 widely comprehensive schools of medium size. For such an exploration I must ask the reader to turn to the next chapter.

CHAPTER TWO

Inequality
of Opportunity

In this and subsequent chapters I shall show the results of the questionnaires sent to the category of
schools I have previously defined. The evidence is clear
that practically all the schools do offer opportunities
that come under the heading of vocational as well as
academic. Therefore in almost all the schools one might
characterize the course offerings as comprehensive.
But by no means do all have as wide an offering as a
comprehensive school should have if it is to do justice
to the desires and potentialities of *all* its students. For
example, in my opinion, every comprehensive high
school should provide instruction in several vocational
fields as well as a diversified list of academic electives.
But to meet such requirements a school board must be
in a position to have a larger staff than would otherwise
be the case. A larger staff means more money. Indeed,
the size of the staff is a fairly accurate measure of the
amount of support a community is willing to give a
school, since salaries for certified professional staff
constitute 70 to 80 per cent of the usual annual school
budget. (The certified professional staff includes all

teachers, counselors, and administrative officers, but *not* the janitorial, custodial, or clerical staff.)

The Educational Policies Commission recommended some years ago that the ratio of certified professional staff to students should be 1 to 20 or less. The answers to our questionnaire show that in the schools responding in our category there is a wide variation in the ratio, from as low as 11.3 to as high as 37.3. One might wonder to what extent the size of the school is a factor in determining the staff-student ratio. An examination of all the returns broken down into three categories according to the school enrollment shows little variation among them, except that there are fewer larger schools (enrollment 1,500–1,999) with a ratio as low as 1 to 17.4 or less, than in the other two enrollment classifications (11.8 per cent as compared with 19.5 and 19.9 per cent for schools with enrollments of 1,000–1,499 and 750–999 respectively). This difference is not large but is contrary to what might have been expected.

Taking all the returns from all the states together, the distribution according to staff-student ratio categories is as follows:

	Ratio students to staff				
	17.4 or less	*17.5–20.4*	*20.5–23.4*	*23.5–26.4*	*26.5 and up*
No. of schools responding	357	680	664	258	60
Per cent of all schools responding	17.6	33.6	32.8	12.7	2.9

Total number of schools reporting: 2,019

TABLE 2. Ratio of students to certified staff in medium-size comprehensive high schools in 31 selected states

	No. of schools	No. of students per single staff member					
		Less than 17.5		17.5–20.4		Total less than 20.5	
		No.	%	No.	%	No.	%
Alabama	23	0	0.0	1	4.3	1	4.3
Arizona	19	0	0.0	11	57.9	11	57.9
California	157	4	2.5	53	33.8	57	36.3
Colorado	23	4	17.4	15	65.2	19	82.6
Connecticut	34	21	61.8	10	29.4	31	91.2
Florida	49	2	4.1	12	24.5	14	28.6
Georgia	49	1	2.0	2	4.1	3	6.1
Illinois	81	21	25.9	38	46.9	59	72.8
Indiana	55	0	0.0	23	41.8	23	41.8
Iowa	19	2	10.5	11	57.9	13	68.4
Kansas	19	2	10.5	7	36.8	9	47.3
Kentucky	27	0	0.0	5	18.5	5	18.5
Louisiana	22	1	4.5	7	31.8	8	36.3
Maryland	31	0	0.0	15	48.4	15	48.4
Massachusetts	72	37	51.4	27	37.5	64	88.9
Michigan	99	1	1.0	28	28.3	29	29.3
Minnesota	41	3	7.3	23	56.1	26	63.4
Missouri	36	5	13.9	14	38.9	19	52.8
New Jersey	133	84	63.2	43	32.3	127	95.5
New York	144	103	71.5	28	19.4	131	90.9
North Carolina	64	0	0.0	8	12.5	8	12.5
Ohio	147	4	2.7	41	27.9	45	30.6
Oregon	31	2	6.5	21	67.7	23	74.2
Pennsylvania	151	24	15.9	70	46.4	94	62.3
South Carolina	28	0	0.0	8	28.6	8	28.6
Tennessee	42	0	0.0	2	4.8	2	4.8
Texas	69	8	11.6	30	43.5	38	55.1
Virginia	63	4	6.3	32	50.8	36	57.1
Washington	55	0	0.0	15	27.3	15	27.3
West Virginia	31	0	0.0	1	3.2	1	3.2
Wisconsin	59	11	18.6	23	39.0	34	57.6
TOTAL	1,873	344	18.4	624	33.3	968	51.7

Total all schools responding from 50 states

	2,019	357	17.7	680	33.7	1,037	51.4

Table 2 lists the percentage of medium-size widely comprehensive high schools (as we have defined them) in each state with staffs sufficient to make the ratio of staff to students 1 to 17.4 or less, or 1 to 20.4 or less.

Only thirty-one states are listed because some states have so few schools in our category that a percentage figure according to the staff-student ratio might be misleading. In the interest of presenting a mass of data as succinctly as possible, we decided to list in all our state-by-state summaries the information from only thirty-one selected states.

One can only contemplate the figures in Table 2 with dismay. On a national basis only 51.4 per cent of the widely comprehensive high schools of medium size are adequately staffed, if one accepts the standard set by the Educational Policies Commission. Or leaving aside anyone's judgment as to a satisfactory staff-student ratio, only just over half the schools under study are as well staffed as 91.2 per cent of the same type of school in Connecticut. Indeed, only 17.7 per cent of all the schools are as well staffed as 61.8 per cent of the schools in Connecticut (ratio 1 to 17.5 or less).

Anyone at all familiar with a public high school of the size and type on which I am reporting would suspect a correlation between the quality of the school and the relative size of the staff. As a matter of fact, we have found such a correlation. To my mind a widely comprehensive high school should as a *minimum* meet the following five criteria:

1. **Provide instruction in calculus;**
2. **Provide instruction in a modern foreign language for four years;**
3. **Arrange the schedule so that a student may study in any one year English, mathematics, science, a foreign language, social studies, physical education, art or music;**
4. **Provide one or more advanced placement courses;**
5. **Have enough English teachers so that "the average pupil load" is 120 or less. (I stand by my recommendation in *The American High School Today* that the student load should be no more than 100, as I make clear later.)**

The following tabulation brings out the correlation between the staff-student ratio and the percentage of the medium-size widely comprehensive schools meeting each of the five criteria.

	Per cent of schools meeting:				
Staff-student ratio	*Criterion* 1	*Criterion* 2	*Criterion* 3	*Criterion* 4	*Criterion* 5
1:17.4 or less	59	88	85	43	58
1:17.5–20.4	38	69	72	30	27
1:20.5–23.4	34	40	62	31	13
1:23.5–26.4	41	45	65	18	10
1:26.5 up	30	48	63	16	10

The reader will note that the first horizontal line of percentages refers to all the schools with a certified professional staff-student ratio of 1 to 17.4 or less, the second refers to those with a ratio of 17.5 to 20.4, and so on. Under each of the column headings is the percentage of all the schools with a given ratio that meet the criterion in question. Thus 59 per cent of all the schools with a ratio of 17.4 or less are offering calculus; 88 per cent are offering four years of a modern foreign language. With all five criteria a higher percentage of the schools with the lower ratio (17.4 or less) is found meeting the criterion than of the schools with a higher ratio.

Another way of summarizing the correlation would be to say that the chances of finding a school that offers calculus, for example, are 59 out of 100 if the staff-student ratio is 1 to 17.4 or less; the chances are only 30 in 100 if the ratio is 26.5 or higher. *If one is seeking any one single criterion to use as the basis for a first approximation to a judgment as to the adequacy of the offerings of a medium-size widely comprehensive school, the certified professional staff-student ratio is to be recommended.* If it is 17.4 or less, the chances are good that the school in question will be adequate in a number of respects.

Unless a principal can boast of a ratio as low as 17.5, he is not likely to be in a position to offer calculus and four years of a modern foreign language or provide adequately for instruction in English composition. I shall present arguments later to support my contention that these five criteria are significant (but not the only significant ones). I postpone further discussion of the educational issues involved in judging the course offerings of a comprehensive high school until later chapters. I wish to conclude this chapter with a brief consideration of the political implications of the data thus far presented.

I have used the word "political" rather than administrative because I wish to focus the attention of the layman who may read these lines on one basic fact— namely, the way we finance our public schools. How much money is available for a school depends on the voters and elective representatives. The decisions are made by state legislatures, local school boards, voters in a school district (in many states), and in recent years by the Congress of the United States. No one can describe in a paragraph the way the responsibility is apportioned in each of the fifty states. No one can describe in even a single chapter the laws and regulations governing the raising of funds and their distribution for public education in a few of the more populous states, let alone all fifty. I have become more and more convinced that one of the main reasons why the financing of our public schools is in such a chaotic state is that no one has presented a clear picture of the situation. Pressure groups and counter pressure groups in Washington, in the state capitals, and locally, are often the main factors. In spite of the importance of education, proclaimed almost daily from the house tops (and political platforms), we have no deep and comprehensive study of the financing of public education state by state. There is not even a nationwide common practice, let alone a national policy. The recently established Education Commission of the States has listed in its agenda, adopted at the first formal meeting, a study of the financing of public schools. Such an inquiry in depth sponsored by a number of state governments through membership on the Education Commission of the States (sometimes referred to as the Compact) should produce alternative suggestions for improving the situation in the several states and clarifying the relationships between Federal, state, and local agencies.

Judging from my many talks about the public schools to lay audiences in recent years and many conversations with private citizens, I am sure not many Americans realize the almost accidental way in which the public schools are financed in most states. A surprisingly small number of otherwise well-informed citizens know that in some states the local school districts receive over two-thirds of the funds from the state, while in other states the figure may be as low as 6 per cent.

By the accidents of the movement of population and of industry, adjacent school districts within a state may differ in their taxable resources by several fold. What one board can afford is out of the question for its neighbor. In those states in which a considerable portion of the expenditures in many districts comes from so-called state aid, the formulas for calculating this aid are so complicated that only the experts can understand them. A public debate on the issue of more or less state aid in such states would be a hopeless undertaking. As I have studied the problems of public secondary education during the last ten years, I have arrived at the conclusion that a radical overhaul of our thinking about financing public schools is required. My prejudices, I am frank to say, are inclining more and more to the belief that the financing of the public schools should be a state and not a local responsibility. As to the role of the Federal treasury, I may as well admit that I am an unreconstructed believer in general Federal aid to public schools. Not that I would fail to applaud the vast amounts of categorical or ear-marked aid that have been supplied by recent acts of Congress. But I believe that a method must be found for apportioning to each of the separate states a share of the funds raised by the Federal Income Tax, to be spent for education as each state sees fit.

Whether the reader agrees with my diagnosis of the financial responsibility of the Congress, the state legislatures, and the local boards, I hope he will consider the evidence presented in this chapter. I realize that many people are tired of hearing the repeated cries of "more money for our schools." Yet I submit that the facts of inequality among schools and among states, as shown by the evidence presented here, cannot be brushed aside. I am not talking in terms of dollars, though the differences between schools with widely different staff-student ratios are ultimately reduceable to dollars. The measure I am using of the adequacy of the support of a school is more significant than the dollar expenditure per pupil. It is independent of the costs of living in the communities in question. It is also independent of the salary scale for teachers, which, to be sure, is far too low in many states.

I invite any citizen who has boasted of our public school system as providing equality of opportunity to ponder on the facts presented in Table 2. If he is a taxpayer in one of the few states in which over half the schools we are considering have a staff-student ratio of 1 to 17.5 or less, he may be inclined to feel proud. But if so, I suggest that as an American he might reflect on what he can do to stir the conscience of his fellow citizens in the other states. I would also suggest that he investigate the extent to which there is equality of educational opportunity among the various school systems within his own state. Facts we have obtained make evident that there are gross inequalities within a state as well as between states. For example, while Massachusetts and Colorado rank high among the states in terms of the percentage of medium-size widely comprehensive schools with a staff-student ratio of less than 20.5 (Table 2), in both states schools exist with a ratio of over 29. In Pennsylvania the minimum ratio is 14.6, but the maximum is 36.4. Altogether, there are five states with at least one school that is badly supported, as shown by its having a ratio higher than 29. It might be pointed out in this connection that since the ratio reflects the cost per pupil, to transform a school whose ratio is 30 to one of 15, would involve almost doubling the budget.

To be sure, the evidence I am presenting refers to only one type of school. It may be that all the public high schools in a given state are well staffed except those that are medium size and widely comprehensive. It is possible but not likely. The fact remains that well over 1,000 schools in the nation are not as well staffed as three-quarters of the same type schools in a few states. Where is the doctrine of equality of opportunity?

The challenge to the leaders of public opinion—indeed to all of the citizens—in those states that show up so badly in Table 2, is self-evident. Likewise the challenge to Federal officials and the Congress of the United States is clear. If a skeptical reader is still unconvinced that our widely comprehensive high schools present a picture of *inequality* of opportunity, I beg him to consider the data in the next two chapters.

CHAPTER THREE

General Education in the High School

I begin by repeating what I said earlier—that the American comprehensive high school has three functions. These are: first, to provide a general education for all the future citizens; second, to provide good elective programs for those who wish to use their acquired skills immediately after graduation; third, to provide satisfactory programs for those whose vocations will depend on their subsequent education in a college or university. After making this statement in *The American High School Today,* I went on to say that "If one could find a single comprehensive high school in the United States in which all these objectives were reached in a highly satisfactory manner, such a school might be taken as a model or pattern." At that time I visited with a few associates a number of schools that had been recommended as highly satisfactory in all three respects. I ended not by naming any one school as a model but by constructing my own model, so to speak, on the basis of the knowledge I had obtained from my visits, and the information provided by teachers and administrators with whom I talked. The model was described in the twenty-one recommendations I addressed to school board members and administrators. "Taken together," I wrote, "they outline the important characteristics of a satisfactory high school which is widely comprehensive." Some of the suggestions corresponded exactly with practices I had found in one or more schools. Others represented ideals that a number of the schools would like to attain.

In this and the next chapter I shall reproduce the text of about half of the recommendations in *The American High School Today*. These are proposals that, if they correspond to present practice in a school, would be reflected in the answers to specific questions in our questionnaire. (I might note that those recommendations not referred to in the following pages were either regarded as of lower priority or as leading to practices which could not be evaluated by a questionnaire. I wish to record that I have not changed my mind about the validity of any of the original twenty-one!) Let me begin with those which are based on a consideration of the first function of a comprehensive high school: to provide for the general education of all the students.

Quite apart from offering adequate instruction in certain fields for all levels of ability, a high school staff should assist each student in the choice of his or her elective program. Without such assistance a youth may choose more often than not courses that are either insufficiently challenging or too demanding. Therefore, a good counseling system, I believe, is basic to the organization of a satisfactory widely comprehensive high school.

THE COUNSELING SYSTEM

The first recommendation in my first report was as follows:

In a satisfactory school system the counseling should start in the elementary school, and there should be good articulation between the counseling in the junior and senior high schools if the pattern is 6–3–3 or between the counseling in the elementary school and the high school if the system is organized on 8–4 basis. There should be one full-time counselor (or guidance officer) for every two hundred fifty to three hundred pupils in the high school. The counselors should have had experience as teachers but should be devoting virtually full time to the counseling work; they should be familiar with the use of tests and measurements of the aptitudes and achievement of pupils. The function of the counselor is not to supplant the parents but to supplement parental advice to a youngster. To this end, the counselor should be in close touch with the parent as well as the pupil. Through consultation, an attempt should be made each year to work out an elective program for the student which corresponds to the student's interest and ability as determined by tests of scholastic aptitude, the recorded achievement as measured by grades in courses and by teachers' estimates. The counselors should be sympathetic to the elective programs which develop marketable skills; they should also understand the program for the slow readers and be ready to cooperate with the teachers of this group of students.

In justifying this recommendation I continued by saying that in some schools the main problem stemmed from the tendency of some academically talented students to avoid courses that required much homework. In other schools the reverse situation was found: the main problem was persuading an overambitious parent of a child with little academic ability that an 11th or 12th grade program must not be too heavily loaded with mathematics, science, and foreign languages. The counselor must recognize the role of adequate motivation, which is difficult to achieve in the case of certain types of students.

THE PRESENT SITUATION

My recommendation called for one full-time counselor (or guidance officer) for every two hundred fifty to three hundred students in the high school. The returns from our questionnaire show that in only 3.4 per cent of the 2,000 schools is the ratio of counselors to students 1 to 249 or less, and that in only 13.9 per cent of the schools is the ratio 1 to 299 or less. In other words, in a vast majority of the schools under consideration my recommendation is far from a reality. Indeed, one has to lower one's standard to a ratio of 1 to 399 or less to accommodate 47.9 per cent of the 2,000 schools on a national basis.

As one studies these figures one is tempted to conclude that in 1959 I was ill-advised. Yet an examination of the summary of the data, state by state in Table 3, may lead to a somewhat different conclusion. Clearly my recommendation corresponds to current practice in only a few comprehensive medium-size schools in many states. Yet if one is willing to increase the desired ratio to 350 students per counselor, then in many states nearly half the schools in question conform to the standard. I do not pretend to be able to evaluate the difference in effectiveness in counseling between a school with a ratio of 1 to 300 and one with a ratio of 1 to 350, but I cannot believe that the staff in a school with only one counselor per 400 students can function as well as a school of a similar type with a hundred less students per counselor. Yet in some states almost no schools in our group have more than one counselor per 400 students, while in others well over 75 per cent are so staffed. I draw two conclusions from these data. First, a thorough, factual study should be made of comparable schools with a ratio of counselors to students of 1 to 300 or less, and 1 to 400 or more. Second, those states in which few of the widely comprehensive medium-size schools have an adequate number of counselors, might well examine their policy. One suspects that the reason for the present situation is not a belief on the part of teachers and administrators that only a relatively few counselors are required, but that the school in question is starved for funds. If the reader will turn back to Table 2 in Chapter 1 and compare it with Table 3, I think this suspicion will be confirmed. By and large the states with a high proportion of schools whose staff ratio corresponds to adequate support are also the states in which a high proportion of schools have an adequate or nearly adequate number of counselors.

Before leaving the subject of the counseling system, I must record that we have examined the relationship between the size of school as measured by enrollment

TABLE 3. Ratio of students to guidance counselors in medium-size comprehensive high schools in 31 selected states by number and per cent of schools

	No. of schools	A Less than 299 No.	A Less than 299 %	B 300–349 No.	B 300–349 %	C 350–399 No.	C 350–399 %	A + B + C Total less than 400 No.	A + B + C Total less than 400 %
Alabama	23	0	0.0	0	0.0	0	0.0	0	0.0
Arizona	19	0	0.0	5	26.3	7	36.8	12	63.2
California	157	12	7.6	36	22.9	39	24.8	87	55.4
Colorado	23	9	39.1	9	39.1	2	8.7	20	87.0
Connecticut	34	9	26.5	7	20.6	7	20.6	23	67.6
Florida	49	1	2.0	2	4.1	3	6.1	6	12.2
Georgia	49	0	0.0	1	2.0	0	0.0	1	2.0
Illinois	81	31	38.3	19	23.5	17	21.0	67	82.7
Indiana	55	5	9.1	17	30.9	21	38.2	43	78.2
Iowa	19	4	21.1	3	15.8	6	31.6	13	68.4
Kansas	19	1	5.3	1	5.3	3	15.8	5	26.3
Kentucky	27	0	0.0	0	0.0	3	11.1	3	11.1
Louisiana	22	2	9.1	0	0.0	0	0.0	2	9.1
Maryland	31	0	0.0	2	6.5	8	25.8	10	32.3
Massachusetts	72	24	33.3	19	26.4	14	19.4	57	79.2
Michigan	99	26	26.3	37	37.4	20	20.2	83	83.8
Minnesota	41	2	4.9	4	9.8	9	22.0	15	36.6
Missouri	37	5	13.5	4	10.8	5	13.5	14	37.8
New Jersey	133	54	40.6	39	29.3	21	15.8	114	85.7
New York	145	38	26.2	51	35.2	23	15.9	112	77.2
North Carolina	66	1	1.5	0	0.0	3	4.5	4	6.1
Ohio	147	10	6.8	13	8.8	25	17.0	48	32.7
Oregon	31	5	16.1	10	32.3	6	19.4	21	67.7
Pennsylvania	151	4	2.6	10	6.6	19	12.6	33	21.9
South Carolina	29	1	3.4	1	3.4	5	17.2	7	24.1
Tennessee	42	5	11.9	1	2.4	1	2.4	7	16.7
Texas	69	1	1.4	2	2.9	4	5.8	7	10.1
Virginia	63	6	9.5	15	23.8	9	14.3	30	47.6
Washington	55	5	9.1	14	25.5	16	29.1	35	63.6
West Virginia	31	0	0.0	0	0.0	0	0.0	0	0.0
Wisconsin	59	6	10.2	9	15.3	8	13.6	23	39.0
TOTAL	1,878	267	14.2	331	17.6	304	16.1	902	48.0

Total all schools responding from 50 states

	2,024	282	13.9	352	17.4	336	16.6	970	47.9

and the proportion of counselors. The size of the school does not appear to be a significant variable.

In my first report I made a distinction between courses that must be satisfactorily completed by all students before graduation (required courses) and the elective offerings. In formulating our questionnaire and interpreting the answers to certain of the questions, we found it difficult to draw a line between required and elective courses. For example, unless one can visit a school and talk with the teachers, it is hard to say whether or not a school requires a course in English every year. Some schools list courses in public speaking, drama, or journalism as English courses: what is significant for evaluation is the content of such courses. Similarly a 9th-grade mathematics course may be part of a four-year sequence or a course in general mathematics. I shall not attempt to assess the extent to which my previous recommendation (number 3, about required programs) corresponds to graduation requirements in the 2,000 schools under scrutiny.

I can report that all but 1 per cent of the schools offer music and all but 14 per cent offer instruction in art. Therefore, essentially all are in a position to influence, through the counseling system, my recommendation that "all students should be urged to include art and music in their elective programs."

ABILITY GROUPING

At the time my first study was made, what is known as "ability grouping" was a highly controversial subject. As I then recorded, "I have met competent teachers who argued vigorously for the heterogeneous grouping in all classes—that is to say, they argued that students of widely different academic abilities and reading skills should be in the same class. Other teachers were equally certain that justice cannot be done to either the bright student or the slow reader if both receive instruction in the same class."

The controversy seems to have subsided, at least in widely comprehensive schools of medium size, for 96.5 per cent of the principals responded affirmatively to the following question: "Do you group students by ability in one or more academic subjects?" However, since there is considerable confusion in many people's minds between ability grouping, subject by subject, and the establishment of "tracks," I repeat recommendation 4 from *The American High School Today.*

In the required subjects and those elected by students with a wide range of ability, the students should be grouped according to ability, subject by subject. For example, in English, American history, ninth-grade algebra, biology, and physical science, there should be at least three types of classes—one for the more able in the subject, another for the large group whose ability is about average, and another for the very slow readers who should be handled by special teachers. The middle group might be divided into two or three sections according to the students' abilities in the subject in ques-

tion. This type of grouping is not to be confused with across-the-board grouping according to which a given student is placed in a particular section in all courses. Under the scheme here recommended, for example, a student may be in the top section in English but the middle section in history or ninth-grade algebra.

Closely related to this recommendation were two others. One, number 8, read as follows:

SPECIAL CONSIDERATION FOR THE VERY SLOW READERS

Those in the ninth grade of the school who read at a level of the sixth grade or below should be given special consideration. These pupils should be instructed in English and the required social studies by special teachers who are interested in working with such students and who are sympathetic to their problems. Remedial reading should be part of the work, and special types of textbooks should be provided.

Nearly 92 per cent of the responses to the questionnaire stated that in the school in question "classes are available for lower ability students." (Our question was made broader than my recommendation concerning slow readers, but in practice the lower ability students with some exceptions would be also slow readers; not all slow readers, however, are students with low ability.)

Another proposal was that a school board should operate a tuition-free summer school in which courses would be available not only for students who had to repeat a subject, but also for the bright and ambitious students who wished to use a summer to broaden the scope of an elective program.

In 80 per cent of the 2,000 schools reporting, a summer school is available; only about 58 per cent of the schools, however, offer instruction in the summer school of the sort that might be classified as "enrichment." Presumably only in these schools would the "bright" and ambitious student find rewarding fare. In general, one may conclude that in our category of schools, summer schools are the rule. Instruction is offered for both the repeater and the able student desirous of getting ahead. Indeed about a third of the responses indicate that "advanced study" is possible in the summer.

SOCIAL STUDIES AND ENGLISH

In a great many public high schools of all types the basis of general education in grades 9 through 12 is sought through social studies and English. One needs no questionnaire to support this generalization. We sought more information about social studies courses and had in mind two of my recommendations of eight years ago. One was incorporated in a recommendation of requirements for graduation and specified that the requirements should include "four years of English, three or four years of social studies—including two years of history (one of which should be American history), and a senior course in American problems or American government." The other expanded the reference to the course in American problems as follows:

In the twelfth grade a course on American problems or American government should be required. This course

should include as much material on economics as the students can effectively handle at this point in their development. Each class in this course should be a cross section of the school: the class should be heterogeneously grouped. Teachers should encourage all students to participate in discussions. This course should develop not only an understanding of the American form of government and of the economic basis of our free society, but also mutual respect and understanding between different types of students. Current topics should be included; free discussion of controversial issues should be encouraged. This approach is one significant way in which our schools distinguish themselves from those in totalitarian nations. This course, as well as well-organized homerooms and certain student activities, can contribute a great deal to the development of future citizens of our democracy who will be intelligent voters, stand firm under trying national conditions, and not be beguiled by the oratory of those who appeal to special interests.

In order to discover to what extent current practices correspond to these recommendations, we asked three questions of the principals: (1) "How many years of social studies are required, grades 9 through 12?" (2) "Is a course in problems in democracy (or equivalent) required?" (3) "If so, do the classes represent a cross section (random selection) of the student body?"

The answers to the first question show that only 3.4 per cent of the schools require one year of social studies, while 28.3 per cent and 43.4 per cent require two and three years respectively. A surprisingly large number (24.9 per cent) require four years. A course in problems in democracy is required in 71 per cent of the

TABLE 4. Number and per cent of medium-size comprehensive high schools in 31 selected states requiring from one to four years of social studies

	No. of schools	One year social studies required No.	%	Two years social studies required No.	%	Three years social studies required No.	%	Four years social studies required No.	%
Alabama	23	0	0.0	2	8.7	18	78.3	3	13.0
Arizona	19	0	0.0	5	26.3	11	57.9	3	15.8
California	157	0	0.0	3	1.9	54	34.4	100	63.7
Colorado	23	2	8.7	5	21.7	11	47.8	5	21.7
Connecticut	34	3	8.8	18	52.9	7	20.6	6	17.6
Florida	49	0	0.0	15	30.6	29	59.2	5	10.2
Georgia	49	0	0.0	1	2.0	45	91.8	3	6.1
Illinois	81	7	8.6	48	59.3	25	30.9	1	1.2
Indiana	55	0	0.0	24	43.6	29	52.7	2	3.6
Iowa	19	1	5.3	8	42.1	4	21.1	6	31.6
Kansas	19	0	0.0	10	52.6	7	36.8	2	10.5
Kentucky	27	0	0.0	21	77.8	4	14.8	2	7.4
Louisiana	22	0	0.0	18	81.8	3	13.6	1	4.5
Maryland	31	0	0.0	2	6.5	17	54.8	12	38.7
Massachusetts	72	13	18.1	26	36.1	23	31.9	10	13.9
Michigan	99	1	1.0	40	40.4	45	45.5	13	13.1
Minnesota	41	0	0.0	1	2.4	6	14.6	34	82.9
Missouri	36	0	0.0	0	0.0	31	86.1	5	13.9
New Jersey	131	0	0.0	90	68.7	35	26.7	6	4.6
New York	145	1	0.7	0	0.0	63	43.4	81	55.9
North Carolina	66	1	1.5	50	75.8	14	21.2	1	1.5
Ohio	147	1	0.7	68	46.3	71	48.3	7	4.8
Oregon	31	0	0.0	4	12.9	23	74.2	4	12.9
Pennsylvania	150	0	0.0	4	2.7	26	17.3	120	80.0
South Carolina	29	0	0.0	17	58.6	11	37.9	1	3.4
Tennessee	42	27	64.3	9	21.4	4	9.5	2	4.8
Texas	69	0	0.0	3	4.3	62	89.9	4	5.8
Virginia	63	0	0.0	3	4.8	50	79.4	10	15.9
Washington	55	0	0.0	4	7.3	36	65.5	15	27.3
West Virginia	31	0	0.0	3	9.7	27	87.1	1	3.2
Wisconsin	59	4	6.8	8	13.6	34	57.6	13	22.0
TOTAL	1,874	61	3.2	510	27.2	825	44.0	478	25.5

Total all schools responding from 50 states

	2,020	69	3.4	571	28.3	877	43.4	503	24.9

schools; 62.5 per cent of the schools indicated that such a course is required and that it is so organized that the classes represent a cross section of the student body. The answers to those two questions about a required course in the problems of democracy are particularly interesting to me, I must confess, as my recommendation has been vigorously attacked. Clearly, in a considerable number of the schools, those who determine policy agree with my appraisal of the value of a course in American problems so organized that a heterogeneous class discusses current issues. It will be noted that my suggestions in regard to the 12th-grade course in American problems is an exception to my general recommendation about "ability groups" (number 4). The reason for the exception is inherent in the recommendation. **1401031**

Let me return now to a discussion of instruction in English for four years as part of the required program. My belief in the importance of devoting so much time each year to English rests largely on my conviction that one of the most important tasks of a high school (of any type) is to improve each student's ability to express himself in writing as well as in speech. On the basis of conversations with teachers during my visits in 1957 and 1958, I became persuaded that half the time spent studying English should be devoted to composition, and that each student should be required to write an average of one theme a week. English teachers believed strongly that, for the best results, themes should be corrected by the regular teacher, who should then discuss them with the students. Adequate instruction requires that teachers not be overloaded. I concluded that English teachers, if they were to perform their function adequately should stand on a different footing from teachers of other subjects. Therefore, the important part of my suggestion concerning English composition (recommendation number 6) read as follows:

"In order that teachers of English have adequate time for handling these themes, no English teacher should be responsible for more than one hundred pupils."

Needless to say, this proposal was welcomed by the teachers of English but not by all the others. A number of experienced administrators disagreed: they objected both to placing the English teachers on a separate footing and to lightening the load of all teachers to 100 students each, which would be too expensive. Furthermore, they pointed out that an alternative method was available. Some administrators have reported success with the use of lay readers. They claim that without reducing the number of students for whom an English teacher is responsible, the teacher's task can be lightened by bringing in laymen to correct the themes. At the time I wrote, the profession was divided on the issue of lay readers.

In view of the strong difference of opinion and my own conclusion in 1959 in favor of increasing the number of English teachers rather than introducing special persons to read themes, I was curious to see what was current practice. Therefore, we asked the following question of all the principals: "What is the average daily load of your English teachers?" The responses show that in very few schools is the load as small as I had proposed (100 students per teacher). However, the principals of 25.5 per cent of the schools report that the load is 119 students or less. Therefore I have taken this figure as one of my minimum criteria. The state-by-state summary of the responses is given in Table 5.

Here, as elsewhere, the data show great differences among states. Thus, on a basis of reports from thirty-one states considered, 73.5 per cent of the schools reporting are staffed with enough English teachers to make the ratio of students to teachers of this subject 139 or less. Yet in some states over half the schools report ratios of 140 students or more per teacher. In three states (Massachusetts, Connecticut, and New York) the majority of schools reporting have enough English teachers to make the average load less than 119 students. It must be emphasized that in each case a local decision about the validity of an educational practice as well as the amount of money available may be at issue. The great differences among schools and among states are clearly evident. What is lacking in our statistics is any information about the use of lay readers in English courses. It may be that a considerable number of the schools in which the number of students per English teacher seems excessive may be using lay readers. Such an explanation of the figures in Table 5 cannot be excluded.

To end this chapter on a positive note I might point out that in 1957–1958 when I examined the instruction in English composition in twenty-one highly recommended comprehensive schools, my initial criterion for a satisfactory ratio was one teacher for 150 or less (*not* my final recommendation, please note). Yet in only about half the schools were there enough English

**TABLE 5. Number of students instructed daily
by one English teacher in medium-size comprehensive high schools
in 31 selected states**

	No. of schools	Less than 99 No.	%	100–119 No.	%	120–139 No.	%	Total less than 140 No.	%
Alabama	23	2	8.7	2	8.7	5	21.7	9	39.1
Arizona	19	0	0.0	4	21.1	9	47.4	13	68.4
California	157	3	1.9	12	7.6	80	51.0	95	60.5
Colorado	23	0	0.0	3	13.0	16	69.6	19	82.6
Connecticut	34	8	23.5	13	38.2	11	32.4	32	94.1
Florida	49	0	0.0	4	8.2	26	53.1	30	61.2
Georgia	49	1	2.0	5	10.2	28	57.1	34	69.4
Illinois	81	7	8.6	32	39.5	35	43.2	74	91.4
Indiana	55	2	3.6	6	10.9	36	65.5	44	80.0
Iowa	19	0	0.0	2	10.5	15	78.9	17	89.5
Kansas	19	0	0.0	3	15.8	10	52.6	13	68.4
Kentucky	27	0	0.0	5	18.5	12	44.4	17	63.0
Louisiana	22	0	0.0	2	9.1	15	68.2	17	77.3
Maryland	31	0	0.0	0	0.0	9	29.0	9	29.0
Massachusetts	72	6	8.3	36	50.0	21	29.2	63	87.5
Michigan	99	4	4.0	8	8.1	53	53.5	65	65.7
Minnesota	41	1	2.4	8	19.5	23	56.1	32	78.0
Missouri	37	0	0.0	4	10.8	21	56.8	25	67.6
New Jersey	132	11	8.3	47	35.6	62	47.0	120	90.9
New York	145	11	7.6	71	49.0	50	34.5	132	91.0
North Carolina	66	1	1.5	4	6.1	41	62.1	46	69.7
Ohio	147	4	2.7	33	22.4	63	42.9	100	68.0
Oregon	31	0	0.0	6	19.4	20	64.5	26	83.9
Pennsylvania	151	3	2.0	30	19.9	65	43.0	98	64.9
South Carolina	29	0	0.0	8	27.6	17	58.6	25	86.2
Tennessee	42	1	2.4	3	7.1	19	45.2	23	54.8
Texas	69	2	2.9	15	21.7	29	42.0	46	66.7
Virginia	63	6	9.5	18	28.6	30	47.6	54	85.7
Washington	55	0	0.0	7	12.7	36	65.5	43	78.2
West Virginia	31	0	0.0	0	0.0	12	38.7	12	38.7
Wisconsin	59	2	3.4	13	22.0	33	55.9	48	81.4
TOTAL	1,877	75	4.0	404	21.5	902	48.0	1,381	73.5

Total all schools responding from 50 states

	2,023	81	4.0	443	21.9	973	48.1	1,497	74.0

teachers to meet this modest criterion. I received the impression then that even under favorable conditions, English teachers would have to cope with as many as 150 pupils. Yet according to the returns I have just been considering, in only 26 per cent of all the schools are there so few English teachers that the average "load" is more than 139 students. I conclude that in all probability courses in English composition are far better staffed than was the case 10 years ago, but many schools still have too few English teachers.

CHAPTER FOUR

The Elective System

I return to the distinction between an elective and a selective system of secondary education. The latter is the characteristic European system; youths who desire to attend a university to study law, medicine, a humanistic, or a scientific discipline are selected at ages ten to twelve and sent to an eight- or nine-year school with little opportunity to choose what they study. The Latin schools in New England at the turn of this century were arranged similarly. They provided a fixed academic curriculum.

The comprehensive high school today, in contrast, offers a variety of courses for a variety of youth with differing interests, desires, and ambitions. It is characterized by opportunities for those who wish to step from high school right into a job, on the one hand, and for those who propose to start the long academic road that starts in the freshman year of a college and terminates in the graduate school of a university.

One of the measures I used in evaluating the comprehensive high schools I visited nearly ten years ago was the adequacy of the courses offered. Was there sufficient variety? Did the instructional programs correspond to the needs of all able and ambitious youths of one sort or another? My judgment then was based on a visit to the school as well as on certain documents I asked the principal to provide. In the present inquiry I can report only on written replies to a questionnaire reviewed by a committee that included several high school administrators. The inventory of course offerings I am presenting in this chapter, though incomplete, has significance because of the number of schools involved. As before, I shall link the reports of the answers to our questions to certain recommendations in *The American High School Today*.

OPPORTUNITIES FOR THE ACADEMICALLY TALENTED

During my visits to schools in 1957–1958, I made a special point of checking the instruction available in mathematics, science, and foreign languages because many critics alleged that a comprehensive school could not meet its obligations in these areas. In every school it was clear from what the teachers said that not all the students were able to handle effectively and rewardingly a program in the 11th and 12th grades that included mathematics, science, a foreign language, English, and social studies. I designated as the "academically talented" those who had the ability to cope with such a program. In a school in which the distribution of academic talent corresponded roughly to the national norm, only about 15 to 20 per cent of the student body in the 9th grade seemed to be in this group.

My conviction as to the courses which the academically talented should be advised to elect was expressed in a recommendation directed to the principal and the counselors. It read as follows:

THE PROGRAMS OF THE ACADEMICALLY TALENTED

A policy in regard to the elective programs of academically talented boys and girls should be adopted by the school to serve as a guide to the counselors. In the type of school I am discussing the following program should be strongly recommended as a minimum:

Four years of mathematics, four years of one foreign language, three years of science, in addition to the required four years of English and three years of social studies; a total of eighteen courses with homework to be taken in four years. This program will require at least fifteen hours of homework each week.

The essence of the recommendation is that students who have the ability to handle effectively both mathematics and a foreign language (by definition, the "academically talented,") should be urged to study both subjects in grades nine through twelve.

To this proposal I added another concerning the *highly gifted*. These students, whose academic talents are highly developed by the time they reach high school, often need special challenges. For them I recommended that courses be provided in the 12th grade as part of the Advanced Placement Program just getting under way. Under this program a student in the 12th grade may take a course of college level in mathematics, English, or history, for example, and, after passing suitable examinations, may receive credit from his college for the courses as well as sophomore standing in these subjects. The very able students may earn as much as one year's credit. The college course can thus be shortened to three years.

The program has proved popular. The numbers involved have grown from a few thousand to over 30,000. In 1965, 107 colleges received 50 or more candidates each, and 188 received 10 to 44 each. Thirty per cent of the 2,000 schools from which we received replies indicate that one or more advanced placement courses are offered. The size of the school in this case is a significant variable. On taking all the returns together one finds that while nearly 40 per cent of the larger schools (enrollment 1,500–1,999) participate in an Advanced Placement Program of one type or another, only 31 per cent of the schools with lower enrollment (1,000–1,499) are involved, and a still smaller fraction (21 per cent) of the smallest schools (enrollment 750–999) in our study participate. These differences did not seem sufficient, however, to make it necessary to complicate a table summarizing the data state by state by introducing categories according to school size.

In Table 6 I have also included a summary by states of the responses to the following question: "Is it possible for a student to take English, mathematics, science, foreign language, social studies, physical education, and art or music within any one year?" This question was prompted by the findings in my first study showing that in many schools, adherence to a six-period-a-day schedule prevented an academically gifted youth from electing a full and challenging program. I was told more than once that if a junior or senior in high school elected the five subjects I advised for those with academic talent, he would not be able to include either art or music if a period must be used in physical education. And physical education every day is often required by state law. With this information before me I advocated in my first report that "the school day be so organized that there are at least six periods in addition to the required physical education and driver education." If this suggestion was followed, a student could study five academic subjects as well as art or music each day. For those who were not able to carry so heavy a load, an extra period was available for another elective in art or music or for study.

The answers are summarized in column 1, Table 6. We did not ask about the organization of the school day because my advisory committee informed me that there has been considerable progress over the last few years in finding alternatives to the rigid restrictions of the six-period day. They have further convinced me that the variations of approach are numerous. The whole situation is in a state of experimentation. To survey the question of school organization would be very difficult, and to make any recommendations would be premature. A separate study devoted exclusively to the organization of the school day would be worthwhile. It should include such approaches as: the ungraded school, modular scheduling, block scheduling, and increased opportunities for independent study.

In other words, the issue is no longer a six-period versus a seven- or eight-period arrangement. In this study, what I wanted to know was whether my suggested program for the bright and ambitious student

TABLE 6. Number and per cent of medium-size comprehensive high schools in thirty-one selected states offering opportunities for advanced academic work

	No. of schools	Students may schedule seven subjects in any one academic year*		Advanced placement program available	
		No.	%	No.	%
Alabama	23	14	60.9	2	8.7
Arizona	19	15	78.9	3	15.8
California	157	114	72.6	42	26.8
Colorado	23	16	69.6	10	43.5
Connecticut	34	28	82.4	19	55.9
Florida	49	31	63.3	15	30.6
Georgia	49	36	73.5	4	8.2
Illinois	81	58	71.6	27	33.3
Indiana	55	41	74.5	14	25.5
Iowa	19	15	78.9	3	15.8
Kansas	19	13	68.4	4	21.1
Kentucky	27	14	51.9	6	22.2
Louisiana	22	13	59.1	8	36.4
Maryland	31	23	74.2	14	45.2
Massachusetts	72	67	93.1	25	34.7
Michigan	99	57	57.6	22	22.2
Minnesota	41	26	63.4	6	14.6
Missouri	37	33	89.2	9	24.3
New Jersey	132	129	97.7	55	41.7
New York	145	140	96.6	70	48.3
North Carolina	66	37	56.1	9	13.6
Ohio	147	121	82.3	47	32.0
Oregon	31	13	41.9	11	35.5
Pennsylvania	151	146	96.7	48	31.8
South Carolina	29	19	65.5	6	20.7
Tennessee	42	27	64.3	4	9.5
Texas	69	28	40.6	32	46.4
Virginia	63	19	30.2	13	20.6
Washington	55	32	58.2	15	27.3
West Virginia	31	19	61.3	10	32.3
Wisconsin	59	49	83.1	14	23.7
TOTAL	1,877	1,393	74.2	567	30.2

Total all schools responding from 50 states

	2,023	1,500	74.1	611	30.2

* School's schedule permits student to take English, science, mathematics, foreign language, social studies, physical education, and art or music in any one year.

was a possible one in the school in question. The questionnaire yielded this information.

In examining Table 6 one must bear in mind that the data presented are useful primarily in showing the present situation state by state as regards the two practices. I believe both are important, but many do not. Those who reject the notion of a heavy academic schedule for one group of students would see no reason why a school should be so organized that seven offerings could be studied. Those who do not believe it wise to anticipate college work in high school would applaud the schools which do *not* participate in the Advanced Placement Program. The fact that there is a fair degree of correlation between the staff-student ratio and the two practices I have recommended cannot be cited as evidence in favor of my proposals. However the correlation does indicate that concern with providing for the development of academic talent often goes hand in hand with an enlargement of the staff.

I was well aware that in making specific recommendations in my first report regarding elective courses in mathematics, science, and a foreign language, I was treading on controversial ground. I expected some teachers, administrators, and professors of education to disagree with me. As it turned out, my expectations were realized. The immediate reaction of a number of the old-timers who had battled against a prescribed curriculum heavily loaded with foreign language and mathematics was to look askance at any suggestion that these subjects as *electives* might have priority for some kinds of students. Yet such was my suggestion.

(I assumed, of course, that English would be a required subject every year and social studies for at least three years.) Foreseeing a negative reaction to my proposals, I attempted to justify my stand by a line of argument I still feel is relevant. I venture to repeat it.

In answering my own question as to why an academically talented student should elect a wide program, I pointed out that if a start were not made toward developing the potentialities of a student in high school, many doors would be closed. For example, a high school graduate who has had no exposure to mathematics or science beyond the 9th grade is going to be in an impossible position if he tries to elect courses *in college* in those subjects. Without realizing it, the advisers of such a boy or girl have foreclosed in high school further exploration of whole areas of knowledge at the college level. Careers in engineering, science, and mathematics become almost inaccessible when the decision has been made in high school to avoid mathematics and science as much as possible.

"If this is true," someone may ask, "why not *require* that all students take the courses you recommend?" The answer I have given several times in the preceding pages. Only in a school that was part of a selective system could any such requirements for a high school diploma be enforced. The essence of a comprehensive school lies in the principle of electives. There are a large number of youths in the kind of school I am considering who are either unwilling or unable to do the amount of work that is implicit in my program for the academically talented. If it is a question only of unwillingness, then, in *theory* at least, the situation might be changed by persuasion of parents, teachers, and counselors. For many, however, it is not lack of desire that precludes the possibility of a study of five academic subjects each of the high school years. Such a program would demand so much burning of the midnight oil as to threaten the health of some individuals. Indeed, I could cite instances in some of the suburban schools I have visited where the present mad rush for entry into prestige colleges has resulted in some students' being subjected to far too heavy a pressure. In such schools boys may be found, for example, enrolled in a course in calculus where they are hopelessly at sea. The failure rate is correspondingly high.

I mention such instances only to show that in trying to challenge able students in an elective system, one is always faced with the possibility of failure in two directions. Too many of those who could but won't, graduate without developing the skills they might; too many aim too high and, in struggling to meet their own or parental aspirations, consume their intellectual energies to little or no avail.

Closely connected with my concern for the programs of the academically able student was a suggestion that the administrators should have information on the extent to which academic courses were being elected by those who could benefit from them. I proposed that a school board, through the superintendent, ask the principal each year to provide an *academic inventory*. Such an inventory, of which I gave examples, summarizes the programs of the academically talented students in the senior class (without giving the names). Admittedly, deciding how to define the group of academically talented is difficult. I suggested using a combination of teachers' judgments and test scores. What one is interested in is the identification of a group, all of whom could handle a heavy academic program if they were sufficiently motivated.

The use of test scores has come under mounting attack since my first report was written. Partly for this reason, partly because it is a laborious task to fill out an academic inventory for a large class, partly because of a lack of understanding of the purpose of the inventory, my proposal has not been favorably received.

In preparing the questionnaire for this second report, it was decided to make no attempt to obtain data that would throw light on the choices made by the academically talented students. It would be difficult to obtain and almost impossible to interpret academic inventories from over 2,000 schools. Therefore in this report I am forced to leave unanswered a highly significant question. I have no way of judging to what degree the schools I am considering are successful in developing the potentialities of their academically talented students. I can only report on the specific opportunities that are present. Whether or not a large proportion of the academically talented in each school take advantage of the opportunities is quite another story. Only a visit to each school and an examination of the individual programs would enable one to come to a conclusion.

Unless one knows what fraction of a grade in a given school has the capacity for a certain type of school work, one cannot evaluate the information on the percentage of those engaged in such work or the study of 12th-grade mathematics or a foreign language. A failure of some prominent laymen to recognize this fact resulted in some highly erroneous judgments about American public schools at the time of the initial Russian success with rockets. It is ridiculous to criticize a school, for example, because only 10 per cent of the senior class had elected 12th-grade mathematics. In some schools, no larger fraction could handle the subject. In others, three times the number might. In short, attempts to interpret enrollments in elective courses may be misleading. I hardly need record that I believe an academic inventory is important. I might add, however, that I am not alone in this opinion. During the years since the idea was first put forward, I am aware that administrators in some schools have prepared academic inventories and found them useful.

FOREIGN LANGUAGES

Perhaps the most discouraging finding in my original study of the comprehensive high school was the inadequacy of the instruction in modern foreign languages. At that time, there seemed to be a widespread feeling among college admission officers and public school administrators that in high school a two-year study of a foreign language was sufficient. As a consequence, it was impossible in many an otherwise adequate school for a student to elect a three- or four-year sequential study of a foreign language. A favorite combination seemed to be two years of Latin and two years of either French or Spanish. The idea that the purpose of studying a foreign language was to gain a mastery of it seemed foreign to many leading educators, yet times were changing. A panel of the National Education Association Conference on the Identification and Education of the Academically Talented held in Washington in February 1958 endorsed the idea of studying a modern foreign language for four years in high school. My own recommendation a year later read as follows:

A school board should be ready to offer a third and fourth year of a foreign language, no matter how few students enroll. The guidance officers should urge the completion of a four-year sequence of *one* foreign language if the student demonstrates ability in handling foreign languages. On the other hand, students who have real difficulty handling the first year of a language should be advised against continuing with the subject. The main purpose of studying a foreign language is to obtain something approaching a mastery of that language, and by a mastery is surely meant the ability to read the literature and, in the case of a modern language, to converse with considerable fluency with an inhabitant of the country in question.

A majority of the school boards in charge of the 2,000 schools on which I am now reporting seems to agree with my recommendation; 64 per cent have arranged to offer instruction in at least one modern foreign language for four years. The situation has clearly changed radically for the better since 1958.

As the data summarized in Table 7 show, however, there is still a majority of medium-size widely comprehensive high schools in some states that do not offer four years of instruction in any modern foreign language. Of course, we have no information as to what the course offering in other types of schools within those states may be. But when one compares the situation state by state one sees how unequal the opportunities are for education in one field, at least, in one prevalent type of school.

I was not unprepared for this radical change in the foreign language situation. When I visited high schools during the past eighteen months, I was constantly reminded of the dramatic change in both the number of years a language might be studied and the number of students electing such programs. The changed climate of opinion concerning the study of foreign languages is well known. It is illustrated by the movement to start the instruction in the lower grades with emphasis on conversation. The introduction of "language laboratories" often provided by Federal funds has accelerated this movement (94 per cent of the 2,000 schools are using the audio-lingual approach). In response to a question of whether the students could begin the study of a foreign language before the 9th grade, 60 per cent of the principals answered in the affirmative. This favorable response does not necessarily mean that the instruction in the lower grades is well articulated with that in grades 9–12. Unfortunately, I have heard evidence to the effect that such coordination may be lacking. Only a visit to the school system in question would yield an answer to this important question.

The size of the school appears to be an important factor in determining whether four years of a foreign language is offered (Table 8). Thus, 43 per cent of the smaller schools (enrollment 750–999) offer four years

TABLE 7. Number and per cent of medium-size comprehensive high schools in thirty-one selected states in which four years of certain languages are offered

	No. of schools	4 years French offered		4 years German offered		4 years Spanish offered		4 years Latin offered	
		No.	%	No.	%	No.	%	No.	%
Alabama	23	1	4.3	0	0.0	1	4.3	1	4.3
Arizona	19	1	5.3	1	5.3	12	63.2	0	0.0
California	157	118	75.2	59	37.6	141	89.8	46	29.3
Colorado	23	18	78.3	8	34.8	17	73.9	7	30.4
Connecticut	34	30	88.2	5	14.7	23	67.6	29	85.3
Florida	49	14	28.6	2	4.1	27	55.1	17	34.7
Georgia	49	12	24.5	2	4.1	12	24.5	10	20.4
Illinois	81	47	58.0	36	44.4	54	66.7	42	51.9
Indiana	55	24	43.6	18	32.7	30	54.5	27	49.1
Iowa	19	11	57.9	1	5.3	14	73.7	6	31.6
Kansas	19	7	36.8	1	5.3	8	42.1	2	10.5
Kentucky	27	6	22.2	1	3.7	6	22.2	6	22.2
Louisiana	22	5	22.7	1	4.5	5	22.7	1	4.5
Maryland	31	30	96.8	2	6.5	20	64.5	18	58.1
Massachusetts	72	67	93.1	12	16.7	27	37.5	49	68.1
Michigan	99	34	34.3	9	9.1	29	29.3	15	15.2
Minnesota	41	16	39.0	19	46.3	11	26.8	3	7.3
Missouri	37	15	40.5	0	0.0	20	54.1	6	16.2
New Jersey	132	121	91.7	90	68.2	114	86.4	96	72.7
New York	145	129	89.0	53	36.6	93	64.1	106	73.1
North Carolina	66	26	39.4	0	0.0	13	19.7	10	15.2
Ohio	147	85	57.8	31	21.1	74	50.3	73	49.7
Oregon	31	19	61.3	14	45.2	23	74.2	6	19.4
Pennsylvania	151	107	70.9	65	43.0	98	64.9	63	41.7
South Carolina	29	10	34.5	2	6.9	6	20.7	7	24.1
Tennessee	42	6	14.3	0	0.0	7	16.7	4	9.5
Texas	69	5	7.2	4	5.8	26	37.7	7	10.1
Virginia	63	34	54.0	7	11.1	32	50.8	34	54.0
Washington	55	25	45.5	15	27.3	26	47.3	7	12.7
West Virginia	31	8	25.8	0	0.0	6	19.4	6	19.4
Wisconsin	59	35	59.3	29	49.2	39	66.1	28	47.5
TOTAL	1,877	1,066	56.8	487	25.9	1,014	54.0	732	39.0

Total all schools responding from 50 states

	2,023	1,140	56.4	504	24.9	1,067	52.7	769	38.0

TABLE 8.   Extent of offerings of French, by years and enrollment, in medium-size comprehensive high schools by number and per cent of schools

Size measured by enrollment	Number of schools	None		One year		Two years		Three years		Four years	
		No.	%	No.	%	No.	%	No.	%	No.	%
750–999	681	88	12.9	5	.7	142	20.9	153	22.5	293	43.0
1,000–1,499	841	40	4.8	3	.4	122	14.5	185	22.0	491	58.4
1,500–1,999	501	12	2.4	0	.0	44	8.8	89	17.8	356	71.1
Total No. and %	2,023	140	6.9	8	.4	308	15.2	427	21.1	1,140	56.3

of French, as compared with 71.1 per cent of the larger schools (enrollment 1,500–1,999) and 58.4 per cent for those in the intermediary range (enrollment 1,000–1,499). Similar data were obtained for the German and Spanish sequences. We decided against further complicating Table 7 by introducing the size of the school as a variable.

MATHEMATICS AND SCIENCE

The changes for the better in the field of modern foreign language instruction have been paralleled by the developments in mathematics and natural science. A movement spearheaded by Professor Zacharias of the Massachusetts Institute of Technology has resulted in new courses in physics, chemistry, and biology. New approaches to mathematics of several varieties were already beyond the experimental stage when I made my visits to the comprehensive high schools nearly a decade ago. We decided in formulating the questionnaire for the present inquiry that we could obtain a significant picture of these new and exciting developments by a few questions. We asked whether the school in question was offering one or more of the new courses in chemistry, physics, and biology (all the schools were offering instruction in these subjects). It turned out that about half of all the schools responding have adopted the new physics, about half the new chemistry, and over a half (64.9 per cent) one of the new biology courses. Thus the evidence is conclusive that those in charge of curricula development in at least half the schools in our category are alert to innovations and have adopted them. I might add that again this supports the impressions I received during my recent visits to schools.

Tables 9A and 9B summarize the returns on a state-by-state basis. I have included in one table the responses to the questions designed to discover whether calculus was offered and whether some other type of advanced mathematics was available. On a national basis 40 per cent of the schools in our category are offering calculus and nearly 23 per cent specified that other types of advanced mathematics could be elected. To anyone interested in developing the academic talent of the nation, these returns are most gratifying. The increase in the number of students who enter college with a knowledge of calculus has delighted some professors of chemistry and physics with whom I have recently talked, though it has meant the organization of a new type of freshman course. The increasing percentage of those who enter college with the particular mathematical skill so important for the natural sciences means

TABLE 9A. Offerings in mathematics in medium-size comprehensive high schools in 31 selected states by number and per cent of schools

	No. of schools	Advanced mathematics offered		Calculus offered	
		No.	%	No.	%
Alabama	23	5	21.7	1	4.3
Arizona	19	3	15.8	10	52.6
California	157	40	25.5	64	40.8
Colorado	23	5	21.7	8	34.8
Connecticut	34	5	14.7	26	76.5
Florida	49	12	24.5	19	38.8
Georgia	49	4	8.2	16	32.7
Illinois	81	30	37.0	31	38.3
Indiana	55	13	23.6	27	49.1
Iowa	19	10	52.6	6	31.6
Kansas	19	8	42.1	9	47.4
Kentucky	27	2	7.4	9	33.3
Louisiana	22	3	13.6	5	22.7
Maryland	31	8	25.8	17	54.8
Massachusetts	72	12	16.7	46	63.9
Michigan	99	12	12.1	27	27.3
Minnesota	41	8	19.5	7	17.1
Missouri	37	11	29.7	10	27.0
New Jersey	132	23	17.4	75	56.8
New York	145	60	41.4	93	64.1
North Carolina	66	9	13.6	15	22.7
Ohio	147	22	15.0	47	32.0
Oregon	31	3	9.7	16	51.6
Pennsylvania	151	33	21.9	79	52.3
South Carolina	29	4	13.8	10	34.5
Tennessee	42	4	9.5	9	21.4
Texas	69	27	39.1	7	10.1
Virginia	63	10	15.9	15	23.8
Washington	55	23	41.8	28	50.9
West Virginia	31	3	9.7	8	25.8
Wisconsin	59	10	16.9	22	37.3
TOTAL	1,877	422	22.5	762	40.6

Total all schools responding from 50 states

	2,023	458	22.6	816	40.3

TABLE 9B. Offerings in "new" sciences in medium-size comprehensive high schools in 31 selected states by number and per cent of schools

	No. of schools	"New" physics offered		"New" chemistry offered		"New" biology offered	
		No.	%	No.	%	No.	%
Alabama	23	8	34.8	7	30.4	10	43.5
Arizona	19	5	26.3	8	42.1	12	63.2
California	157	103	65.6	108	68.8	136	86.6
Colorado	23	15	65.2	16	69.6	22	95.7
Connecticut	34	20	58.8	13	38.2	18	52.9
Florida	49	40	81.6	32	65.3	44	89.8
Georgia	49	15	30.6	17	34.7	35	71.4
Illinois	81	45	55.6	45	55.6	59	72.8
Indiana	55	18	32.7	18	32.7	29	52.7
Iowa	19	11	57.9	10	52.6	14	73.7
Kansas	19	13	68.4	14	73.7	14	73.7
Kentucky	27	7	25.9	5	18.5	12	44.4
Louisiana	22	8	36.4	4	18.2	9	40.9
Maryland	31	22	71.0	14	45.2	26	83.9
Massachusetts	72	50	69.4	48	66.7	54	75.0
Michigan	99	42	42.4	39	39.4	58	58.6
Minnesota	41	25	61.0	25	61.0	27	65.9
Missouri	37	14	37.8	12	32.4	21	56.8
New Jersey	132	87	65.9	69	52.3	82	62.1
New York	145	51	35.2	58	40.0	69	47.6
North Carolina	66	21	31.8	17	25.8	40	60.6
Ohio	147	55	37.4	60	40.8	75	51.0
Oregon	31	26	83.9	25	80.6	27	87.1
Pennsylvania	151	70	46.4	74	49.0	97	64.2
South Carolina	29	8	27.6	9	31.0	15	51.7
Tennessee	42	6	14.3	9	21.4	14	33.3
Texas	69	28	40.6	26	37.7	46	66.7
Virginia	63	22	34.9	20	31.7	40	63.5
Washington	55	47	85.5	40	72.7	51	92.7
West Virginia	31	12	38.7	15	48.4	11	35.5
Wisconsin	59	36	61.0	36	61.0	45	76.3
TOTAL	1,877	930	49.5	893	47.6	1,212	64.5

Total all schools responding from 50 states

	2,023	1,001	49.5	962	47.6	1,312	64.9

that many freshmen can continue their study of science on a more sophisticated basis than in the past. A generation ago it was almost unheard of for a high school to include calculus among the subjects that could be studied. For the future student of the social sciences, a 12th-grade course in statistics may be more important than calculus. There is no reason why the list of electives should not include both, which seems to be the case in a number of the schools under investigation.

VOCATIONAL EDUCATION

When I wrote *The American High School Today,* I was fairly certain as to how a state should provide vocational education. Today I am not so certain. On the one hand, in some large cities, vocational schools are becoming widely comprehensive schools. In some states, on the other hand, area vocational schools are being established. Whether these are to be entirely post–high school or involved in instruction in grades 11 and 12 is not yet certain. But as a starting point let me repeat my earlier recommendation addressed to those in charge of widely comprehensive high schools. It ran as follows:

DIVERSIFIED PROGRAMS FOR THE DEVELOPMENT OF MARKETABLE SKILLS

Programs should be available for girls interested in developing skills in typing, stenography, the use of clerical machines, home economics, or a specialized

branch of home economics which through further work in college might lead to the profession of dietician. Distributive education should be available if the retail shops in the community can be persuaded to provide suitable openings. If the community is rural, vocational agriculture should be included. For boys, depending on the community, trade and industrial programs should be available.

Let us see what the responses to our questionnaire indicate about the kind of vocational courses offered in the widely comprehensive schools we were questioning. In the first place, 92.4 per cent of all the schools that reported list a course in business education and nearly 90 per cent a course in home economics. It is on the basis of these returns that one may say that practically all the 2,000 schools offer a comprehensive program. However, it can be argued that a school in which there is so limited a range of vocational electives does not meet the test of providing courses for a variety of interests. One of my criteria for judging the adequacy of a widely comprehensive school would be the offering, in addition to courses in business education and home economics, of instruction in auto mechanics or building trades. Those schools reporting instruction in auto mechanics or building trades or closely related offerings amount to 70 per cent. Table 10 summarizes on a state-by-state basis the information we received in response to questions about auto mechanics, building trades, distributive education, agriculture, and work-study programs. A categorization of all the returns into three groups according to enrollment shows almost no

TABLE 10. Number and per cent of medium-size comprehensive high schools in 31 selected states offering vocational instruction—by subject categories

	No. of schools	Auto mech.		Bldg. trades		Dist. ed.		Agriculture		Co-op work-study prog.		Othe voc. st
		No.	%	No.	%	No.	%	No.	%	No.	%	No.
Alabama	23	7	30.4	5	21.7	18	78.3	7	30.4	17	73.9	7
Arizona	19	9	47.4	13	68.4	12	63.2	9	47.4	7	36.8	3
California	157	128	81.5	74	47.1	76	48.4	73	46.5	98	62.4	50
Colorado	23	17	73.9	11	47.8	17	73.9	6	26.1	11	47.8	12
Connecticut	34	17	50.0	16	47.1	15	44.1	4	11.8	16	47.1	11
Florida	49	19	38.8	19	38.8	44	89.8	24	49.0	37	75.5	17
Georgia	49	11	22.4	14	28.6	25	51.0	22	44.9	22	44.9	19
Illinois	81	41	50.6	24	29.6	33	40.7	34	42.0	50	61.7	25
Indiana	55	31	56.4	20	36.4	24	43.6	20	36.4	25	45.5	16
Iowa	19	17	89.5	11	57.9	15	78.9	2	10.5	15	78.9	10
Kansas	19	15	78.9	8	42.1	10	52.6	9	47.4	10	52.6	11
Kentucky	27	11	40.7	10	37.0	11	40.7	16	59.3	12	44.4	9
Louisiana	22	8	36.4	12	54.5	12	54.5	3	13.6	10	45.5	4
Maryland	31	22	71.0	11	35.5	8	25.8	8	25.8	12	38.7	13
Massachusetts	72	34	47.2	30	41.7	20	27.8	2	2.8	27	37.5	22
Michigan	99	66	66.7	35	35.4	73	73.7	31	31.3	75	75.8	40
Minnesota	41	14	34.1	19	46.3	28	68.3	22	53.7	24	58.5	10
Missouri	37	22	59.5	14	37.8	29	78.4	13	35.1	27	73.0	16
New Jersey	132	78	59.1	39	29.5	48	36.4	16	12.1	75	56.8	51
New York	145	97	66.9	58	40.0	94	64.8	27	18.6	98	67.6	47
North Carolina	66	21	31.8	32	48.5	49	74.2	39	59.1	36	54.5	26
Ohio	147	66	44.9	32	21.8	84	57.1	25	17.0	82	55.8	54
Oregon	31	12	38.7	15	48.4	15	48.4	18	58.1	18	58.1	9
Pennsylvania	151	59	39.1	49	32.5	34	22.5	51	33.8	51	33.8	42
South Carolina	29	12	41.4	14	48.3	20	69.0	17	58.6	15	51.7	19
Tennessee	42	10	23.8	14	33.3	23	54.8	16	38.1	14	33.3	16
Texas	69	30	43.5	21	30.4	59	85.5	46	66.7	36	52.2	27
Virginia	63	20	31.7	25	39.7	52	82.5	23	36.5	45	71.4	28
Washington	55	43	78.2	27	49.1	40	72.7	22	40.0	20	36.4	14
West Virginia	31	11	35.5	6	19.4	7	22.6	11	35.5	7	22.6	11
Wisconsin	59	24	40.7	34	57.6	15	25.4	25	42.4	22	37.3	19
TOTAL	1,877	972	51.8	712	37.9	1,010	53.8	641	34.2	1,014	54.0	658

Total all schools responding from 50 states

	2,023	1,056	52.2	787	38.9	1,084	53.6	696	34.4	1,095	54.1	715

variation in the percentage offering building trades and not as great a variation as might have been expected in auto mechanics (42 per cent, 53 per cent, and 64 per cent in the increasing order of size).

Since 1959, when my first report appeared, much has been written about vocational education, and the basis for the expenditure of Federal funds in this area has been altered and expanded. Therefore, some of the sentences in my original recommendation are no longer valid. They have been omitted in the quotation given above. Only by visiting a number of schools with wide vocational programs could one hope to evaluate the present situation. What the data in Table 10 demonstrate is that in at least half the schools in question, vocational instruction is offered in one or more fields besides business education and home economics. We are dealing, therefore, in such schools with a widely comprehensive list of offerings. This fact is significant for our findings in regard to the academic elective courses. In many of the schools under review, the courses are as diversified as one might hope to find. There is no evidence that instruction in vocational courses has interfered with instruction in advanced academic fields. On the contrary, we found that of the schools offering calculus, 70 per cent also offer courses in either auto mechanics or building trades. So an opportunity is present both for the boy who wants to earn a living working with his hands and is ready to take a job on graduation, and also for the future engineer who must first enter an engineering school and should study 12th-grade mathematics.

From time to time during the past decade proposals

have been put forward to move instruction in auto mechanics, building trades, and machine shop work to a post–high school technical institute or junior college. Less radical changes involve the establishment of a high school with facilities for vocational work that would serve a number of high schools. Some such arrangements are in force in several areas. The high school senior (and perhaps junior) travels by bus in order to obtain vocational instruction during part of a day. There are so many proposals and so many changes in the whole field of vocational education that it would be worse than useless for me to attempt a diagnosis, let alone a prognosis. I would like to repeat a conviction I acquired ten years ago, which recent discussions still have not altered. In *The American High School Today* I formulated it as follows:

My inclination is strongly in favor of including vocational work in a comprehensive high school instead of providing it in a separate high school. My reasons are largely social rather than educational. I believe it is important for the future of American democracy to have as close a relationship as possible in high school between the future professional man, the future craftsman, the future manager of industry, the future labor leader, the future salesman, and the future engineer. As I have often stressed in my writings and earlier in this report, I am convinced that one of the fundamental doctrines of American society is equality of status in all forms of honest labor as well as equality of opportunity.

To my mind, it is desirable for as many boys and girls in high school as possible to have an ultimate vocational goal. It may well be that many of them will change their minds before the high school course is over or in later years. But if a student thinks that what he or she is studying in school is likely to have significance in later life, the study in question takes on a new importance. There is less tendency for such "committed" students to waste their time or have a negative attitude toward their schoolwork.

An argument along the same lines applies in a discussion of whether or not vocational instruction should be postponed to the immediate post–high school years. Granted the tremendous expansion of public facilities for education at the junior college level and granted that better instruction might be offered in a two-year college or technical institute than in a high school, the problem of motivation of certain types of youth still remains. In every community of any size there are some of high school age who, for one reason or another, regard formal education as at best a bore. Better teaching and smaller classes can reduce this number. The ambition of the parents and the neighbors play a large role in many cases. I am sure, however, that an appreciable percentage of this type of student remains in school with some enthusiasm because attractive opportunities for vocational education are provided. Moving these facilities to another institution would remove a motivating force. Many experienced administrators in comprehensive high schools with whom I discussed these problems have agreed.

If the high school in question is located in a community where a sufficient number of boys desire some instruction in a skilled trade, then the widely comprehensive high school is still the answer. But in many school districts in many states, the condition I have just specified does not exist. Such is the case in suburban schools where more than 75 per cent (often more than 90 per cent) of the boys want to enter a four-year college. How the state should provide for the development of skills "marketable" upon graduation under such circumstances is a question to which I have no firm answer. Nor am I prepared to say just how a state can provide vocational instruction in these schools when it is desired by only a few. Much has changed in the last ten years. The indications are that even more chaotic changes are in store. With a brief consideration of what lies ahead I conclude this report with a final chapter.

CHAPTER FIVE

Public Education Today and Tomorrow

Public education today is usually thought of as divided into three levels: elementary, secondary, and higher. Elementary schools and high schools are almost without exception the responsibility of local boards of education. Public higher education is organized with boards of trustees, each one as a rule responsible for a single institution. In the past the line between high school and a four-year college as part of a university was hard and fast. With the growth of the two-year college, the relationship between the high school and college is becoming more complicated. At the conclusion of this chapter I shall look into the future and consider the changing pattern of public education. Before doing so, let me attempt to summarize the results of our investigation and their implications for the financing of public secondary education.

Table 11, which is divided into two parts, summarizes much of what has been said in the preceding four chapters and, in addition, provides information on certain combinations of the criteria. Since I am concerned with the comprehensive nature of the high

TABLE 11. Summary of findings

A. Individual criteria and certain combinations

Criteria		Percentage of 2,000 schools
1.	Instruction in calculus	40.0
2.	Four years of one modern foreign language	65.0
3.	School so organized that five academic subjects plus art or music and physical education may be studied in one day	74.2
4.	Courses in the Advanced Placement Program available	30.2
°5.	Ratio of English teachers to students studying English, 1 to 120 or less	25.8

	Per cent of schools meeting all five of the above criteria	10.8	
	Schools meeting first four of above criteria	13.2	
	Schools meeting criteria 1, 2, 3, and 5	21.4	
	Schools meeting first two criteria	31.8	

6.	Three years of social studies required	43.4
7.	Course in auto mechanics or building trades	52.2

	Per cent of schools meeting criteria 1, 2, 6, and 7 (instruction in calculus, four years of one modern foreign language, three years of required social studies, course in auto mechanics or building trades)	15.3	
	Per cent of schools meeting criteria 1, 2, and 7 (instruction in calculus, four years of one foreign language, auto mechanics or building trades)	21.7	
	Per cent of schools meeting criteria 1 and 7 (instruction in calculus, auto mechanics or building trades)	27.9	

B. Summary of other findings

Criteria	Percentage of 2,000 schools
8. Ratio of certified professional staff to students of 1 to 20.4 or less	51.2
°9. Ratio of counselors to students of 1 to 349 or less	31.5
10. New physics, chemistry, or biology	64.9
11. Instruction in advanced mathematics other than calculus	22.6
12. Course in problems of democracy with heterogeneous classes	62.5
13. Course in distributive education	53.6
14. Summer school	80.1
15. Course for slow learners	91.9
16. Students grouped by ability in at least one course	96.5
17. Course in business education	92.4
18. Course in home economics	88.8
19. Instruction in music	98.8
20. Instruction in art	94.3

° These criteria represent a somewhat different standard from that set by the recommendations in *The American High School Today.*

schools we are examining, I attach particular significance to the combination of criteria of an academic type (first five, Table 11) and the offering of auto mechanics or building trades (item 7, Table 11). (It will be recalled that we chose those two headings as representing vocational opportunities.) Anyone who challenges the offerings in these schools as not being widely comprehensive should note from Table 11 that over 90 per cent of the schools offer courses in business education and nearly 90 per cent in home economics. Perhaps one might say that if a school is going to be comprehensive it should offer, at the very least, a strong program in one subject on the academic side and one subject on the vocational side. With this in mind we asked questions that brought out the following fact: 60 per cent of the schools reporting offer auto mechanics, building trades, or closely related subjects *and* either calculus or four years of one modern foreign language.

Table 11 is essentially self-explanatory. It might be pointed out, however, that the larger the number of criteria applied in judging a school, the fewer the schools that will meet the standard. Although only 10.8 per cent of the schools meet all five criteria listed in Chapter 2, nevertheless 31.8 per cent offer both four years of one modern foreign language and calculus. One additional fact not hitherto reported should be added—that 45.7 per cent of the schools reporting offer four years of two foreign languages. It seems quite certain that there is little connection between the spread of 1965 graduates entering post–high school institutions (25–74 per cent) and the vast improvement and extension in foreign language and mathematics offerings.

Because the comprehensive high school has so often been attacked as providing inadequate opportunities for the bright students, I have in both my first and

second reports emphasized opportunities that should
be available to those who are going on to college and,
perhaps later, to professional school. One can conclude
that in the ten years since I made my first study, considerable progress has been made in the teaching of
mathematics, science, and foreign languages. Indeed,
the situation regarding mathematics may be better than
the findings in Table 11 indicate. Schools that offer
advanced mathematics other than calculus may provide
as satisfactorily for certain types of academically talented youth as those that offer calculus. Therefore, one
might claim that something like 60 per cent of the
schools are satisfactory in 12th-grade mathematics.
Someone reading our findings with a critical eye might
say, "Well, of course, the schools that provide so well
for the ambitious and bright students are the schools
among your 2,000 from which well over 50 per cent
are going on to college." In order to examine this possible criticism, we divided our schools into three groups
corresponding to the percentage of 1965 graduates
proceeding with further education. One group included
those schools from which 25–39 per cent proceeded,
the next, 40–59 per cent, and the third, 60–75 per cent.
We found that the middle group, which represents
roughly 50 per cent going on to college, has as high a
percentage of schools offering a strong academic program as does the group of schools from which 60 to 75
per cent proceeded. These results largely answer my
hypothetical critic's objection. This is important. It
might well have turned out that the good showing in
foreign languages and calculus for the entire 2,000
schools was a consequence of a high percentage of

academic offerings in those schools sending more than 60 per cent to college. But this is not the case. It seems quite certain that the vast improvement in foreign languages and mathematics is almost independent of the percentage of 1965 graduates who are continuing their education.

Before going on to a consideration of what lies ahead, let me emphasize the significance of the data in Table 11 and our findings on the percentage of schools meeting different groups of my criteria. Whether one is encouraged or discouraged by contemplating these findings depends largely on one's expectation and one's judgment of what is important in secondary education. Had a similar compilation been possible ten years ago, Table 11 would show that American public education has been improving, but is yet far below the level I think it can reach before long.

THE NEW TECHNOLOGY

One important finding I have not yet reported. I am frank to say that it surprised me and will surprise even more some of my acquaintances who have been deeply involved in what are called the new technological innovations. Only 10.9 per cent of the principals who replied to our questionnaire indicate that television is a major teaching device in one or more subjects, and only 16.2 per cent report the use of programmed instruction. Indeed, more than one principal volunteered the information that he had tried programmed instruction and abandoned it.

I am sure that those who are most familiar with the so-called technological revolution in education will be quick to point out that these results are to be expected at the beginning of a revolutionary era. Indeed, some might attribute them to the conservatism of the high school principal. This seems to me an unlikely explanation, however, since 64.9 per cent of the principals replied that they have adopted either the new physics, the new chemistry, or the new biology. Furthermore, the information already compiled on foreign languages indicates how ready the principals are for innovations (Chapter 4); 94 per cent of the 2,000 schools reported that they are using the audio-lingual approach. It is a significant fact that 60 per cent of the principals responded that their students had begun this type of program before the 9th grade.

Regarding television, it seems possible that before too long a classroom teacher can have at his disposal the equivalent of a library of instructional material. From such a library, he can choose to show on a television receiver or receivers, for as short or as long periods as desired, either portions of a sequential course or supplementary material. The flexibility of such arrangements would seem to open up new prospects for the use of television as an aid to learning. Similar photographic devices are also in the offing. Admittedly, there are problems. The financing of the production and distribution of the tapes or their equivalent that are to constitute a school library should be of national concern. In principle, the situation is no different from the publication of textbooks, but the initial costs are extraordinarily high. It is hardly to be expected that a multitude of first-rate competing "television tapes" will be forthcoming in the immediate future.

If one envisages the school library transformed into a center for various resources for promoting learning, one realizes this is only a continuation of the characteristic American emphasis on the school library. It is unnecessary to emphasize that the American public high school in recent years has built much of its instruction around a library of sufficient size. In my experience European educators have no conception of the proper role of a library in the instruction of youth. Few citizens realize the significance of this distinctive feature of the American schools as compared with those in other countries. The change has come about in the course of my lifetime. The library of the selective Latin school from which I graduated in 1910 could be placed on one shelf alongside the dictionary and the *Encyclopaedia Britannica.*

The smallest school in our category has an enrollment of 750. I have been told by experts that such a school should have a minimum of 7,500 books in its library collection. In our questionnaire, we asked about the number of books in the school library. The results are tabulated in Table 12.

It will be noted that 40 per cent of all the schools do not meet our minimum standard. As we contemplated the returns, however, we became more and more aware of the difficulties in obtaining significant data about school libraries. Some of the members of the committee, who are immersed daily in the problems of high school management, pointed out that some school libraries consist to a considerable extent of duplicates or

TABLE 12. Number of volumes in the libraries of medium-size comprehensive high schools by categories and size of schools

Size measured by enrollment	Number of schools	0–7499 volumes		7,500–9,999 volumes		10,000–14,999 volumes		15,000+ volumes	
		No.	%	No.	%	No.	%	No.	%
750–999	678	400	59.0	157	23.2	111	16.4	10	1.5
1000–1499	836	328	39.2	254	30.4	217	26.0	37	4.4
1500–1999	501	80	16.0	134	26.7	219	43.7	68	13.6
TOTAL	2,015	808	40.1	545	27.0	547	27.1	115	5.7

obsolete books. Therefore, our findings in regard to the size of the library collection can only be considered as a first approximation of a meaningful assessment. Furthermore, we have made no attempt to examine three important aspects of the utility of libraries—the accessibility of the volumes, the seating space in the library, and the influence of the library on the students and the faculty.

Quite apart from the new kind of library in tomorrow's schools, the development of which depends on the improved use of audio-visual aids to learning, one hears of an impending revolution to be brought about by a vast improvement in programmed instruction. Computers and other forms of new hardware are to be introduced. If I understand the enthusiastic proponents of the new technology, it is claimed that many students who now have difficulty with mathematics and foreign languages will be able to handle these subjects as well as do the academically talented. If and when the happy day arrives when the predictions of the educational revolutionists are realized, some of the distinctions

I have made between the academically talented and the others will disappear. In terms of academic talent, the spectrum of the comprehensive high school will be shifted toward the highly gifted. The chief variable in school learning would then be less the ability of the student than his desire to learn. Indeed, as progress is made toward the ideal situation, more and more emphasis will be placed on motivation. If all the youth in a high school could gallop through their studies at the same rate as the ablest today, if all were motivated by the same drive, the same zest for learning as the most ambitious, if one can imagine such an ideal situation in terms of school learning, then attention could be focused on the social ideals of a widely comprehensive school: the reduction of the degree of misunderstanding and prejudice among families with a variety of ethnic, economic, and religious backgrounds. In short, I can see that the essential elements in the concept of the widely comprehensive American secondary school may become more important as teaching problems are solved.

BEYOND THE HIGH SCHOOL

A significant change in American public education has been taking place that has nothing to do with the innovations I have been discussing. It is a revolution nonetheless. I refer to the expansion of the two-year colleges and technical institutes. I have already referred to the evidence from our questionnaire that points to the rapidly growing success of the Advanced Placement

Programs. To be sure, only about a third of the schools responding were offering advanced placement courses. Furthermore, the students involved were for the most part the highly gifted academically. Nonetheless the innovation points to a breaking down of the old barrier between high school and college. The growth of the local two-year college or technical institute seems to me to be part of the same picture. Public education is spreading upward in many states. On this point, the answers to some of the questions on our questionnaire provide interesting information.

In 1965 over half of the graduates (nearly 56 per cent) of all the schools responding enrolled in either a four-year college, a two-year college, or a technical institute. Of those going on, however, by no means all entered a four-year institution, as would have been the case a generation or two ago. On the contrary, over a third of those continuing entered a two-year college or a technical institute. In other words nearly 21 per cent of the high school graduates continue in some institution other than a four-year college. The projection of the growth of local two-year colleges in many states indicates that in another decade a large proportion of those who finish high school are going to go right ahead with formal education locally.

One begins to speak of grades 13 and 14 as part of our system of public education. Table 13 summarizes some of the data yielded by the returns from our questionnaire. As would be expected, the facts reveal how different the situation is state by state, yet how uniform is the total per cent of those going on (49.1–68.2).

TABLE 13. Number and per cent of 1965 graduates who entered four-year colleges, junior colleges, and technical or other post-secondary schools from medium-size public comprehensive secondary schools in 31 selected states

	No. of schools	No. 1965 graduates	Four-year college	%	Junior college	%	Technical & other schools	%	Total graduates continuing	% graduates continuing
Alabama	23	7,400	2,998	40.5	678	9.2	425	5.7	4,101	55.4
Arizona	19	4,643	1,506	32.2	898	19.3	247	5.3	2,651	57.0
California	157	51,184	9,232	18.0	19,131	37.4	2,869	5.6	31,232	61.0
Colorado	23	7,605	3,386	44.5	963	12.7	342	4.5	4,691	61.6
Connecticut	34	11,591	4,536	39.1	813	7.0	1,763	15.2	7,112	61.3
Florida	49	17,635	4,380	24.8	5,300	30.1	1,072	6.1	10,752	60.9
Georgia	49	12,307	4,226	34.3	1,643	13.4	1,309	10.6	7,178	58.3
Illinois	81	24,991	10,160	40.7	2,107	8.4	1,843	7.4	14,110	56.5
Indiana	55	16,136	6,312	39.1	151	.9	1,462	9.1	7,925	49.1
Iowa	19	8,303	2,447	29.5	1,448	17.4	743	8.9	4,638	55.8
Kansas	19	5,855	2,467	42.1	929	15.9	598	10.2	3,994	68.2
Kentucky	27	7,200	2,837	39.4	410	5.7	523	7.3	3,770	52.4
Louisiana	22	6,683	3,654	54.7	68	1.0	424	6.3	4,146	62.0
Maryland	31	12,323	4,076	33.1	1,709	13.9	789	6.4	6,574	53.3
Massachusetts	72	22,939	6,857	29.9	1,845	8.0	3,868	16.9	12,570	54.8
Michigan	99	30,299	9,462	31.2	3,480	11.5	2,188	7.2	15,130	49.9
Minnesota	41	14,528	5,533	38.1	1,309	9.0	1,746	12.0	8,588	59.1
Missouri	37	12,340	4,929	39.9	1,173	9.5	458	3.7	6,560	53.1
New Jersey	133	43,014	16,760	39.0	1,430	3.3	5,325	12.4	23,515	54.6
New York	145	44,878	15,063	33.6	5,018	11.2	5,702	12.7	25,783	57.5
N. Carolina	66	16,941	6,500	38.4	1,124	6.6	2,587	15.3	10,211	60.2
Ohio	147	46,583	17,980	38.6	1,309	2.8	3,621	7.8	22,910	49.1
Oregon	31	11,498	4,178	36.3	1,049	9.1	828	7.2	6,055	52.6
Pennsylvania	151	48,771	15,858	32.5	2,112	4.3	6,710	13.8	24,680	50.6
S. Carolina	29	7,820	3,213	41.1	405	5.2	701	9.0	4,319	55.2
Tennessee	42	11,083	4,647	41.9	242	2.2	698	6.3	5,587	50.4
Texas	69	20,901	9,079	43.4	3,215	15.4	1,482	7.1	13,776	65.9
Virginia	63	15,897	6,211	39.1	1,003	6.3	1,474	9.3	8,688	54.7
Washington	55	22,841	6,583	28.8	5,853	25.6	1,452	6.4	13,888	60.8
W. Virginia	31	9,111	4,260	46.8	133	1.5	579	6.4	4,972	54.6
Wisconsin	59	18,307	7,080	38.7	354	1.9	2,577	14.1	10,011	54.7
TOTAL	1,878	591,607	206,410	34.8	67,302	11.4	56,405	9.5	330,117	55.7

For example, in California, a state in which the local two-year college has been well developed for a number of years, only 18 per cent of the graduates of whom we are talking entered a four-year college; about 37.4 per cent enrolled in two-year colleges, and the remainder in technical institutes. In Indiana, on the other hand, nearly 40 per cent of the graduates entered four-year institutions. But in reading these figures one must remember that here, as well as in some other states, the four-year public university provides instruction in the first two years at a number of different places within the state. There are differences in the organization of public instruction in those states where separate public junior colleges exist (as in California), and in other states where the four-year public university provides extension of its work locally. It is no part of this study, however, to examine these differences or attempt to evaluate the various arrangements. Perhaps the most significant findings are the comparisons state by state of the percentage of graduates of schools in our category who go on to either a four-year or two-year institution. A surprising outcome of the replies to our questionnaire was the fact that there is very little difference between the statistics for men and women (Table 14).

The time may come when it will be the rule for a state to envision the task of educational authorities as the planning of a fourteen-year course of study for all or almost all youth. I can imagine that under such circumstances the present vocational courses might be displaced to grades 13 and 14. My "open door" argument, on the advisability of a student's electing sequen-

TABLE 14.   Percentage of boy and girl 1965 graduates continuing post-secondary school education (50 states)

	Four-year college	Junior college	Technical and other schools	Total
Boys	37.5	12.0	8.4	57.6
Girls	33.2	10.0	10.6	53.6
Total boys and girls	35.3	11.0	9.5	55.6

tial courses in mathematics and foreign languages, would be recast in terms of alternate programs starting in grade 10 and running through grade 14.

In conjuring up various forecasts of the future of public education one must not overlook the possibility of structural changes, such as a redrafting of district lines and the shifting of the financial basis for instruction in grades 9 through 14. It is useless for me to try to list the alternatives that may emerge on the changing scene. One point only I should like to emphasize. Whatever alternatives may seem advisable in providing the best instruction, due weight must be given to the social factor that is so prominent in arguments in favor of the comprehensive high school. Today there can be no question that the American people subscribe to the doctrine that public schools should operate within an *elective* and not a *selective* framework. It is well to remember that according to the returns from our first questionnaire, only 7 per cent of all the more than 15,000 public high schools responding send more than 75 per cent of the graduates on to college. Even those public schools that are in fact like selective schools (because of the ambitions of suburban families) are a small minority. The movement to extend free (or almost free) education upwards to grades 13 and 14 locally is equivalent to moving upwards the concept of a comprehensive institution. The four-year institutions, whether private or public, have become increasingly selective in recent years. Usually the local two-year college continues the broad range of course offerings of the comprehensive high school. It may be that in another decade it will not be the high school that should be reviewed in many states but the instruction available at low cost for grades 9 to 14. In that case, at least some of the questions raised in my first report and some of my recommendations should be addressed *not* to high school principals alone. It would seem appropriate for the chief state school officer in each state to institute from time to time an inquiry of the entire fourteen years of public education. Then one would have a clearer picture of the opportunities offered throughout the nation. I venture to hope that the mere process of undertaking such an inquiry would be a move toward overcoming the gross educational inequalities that stand out so clearly in the preceding pages.

Perhaps more important for public education tomorrow than the innovations I have been considering is the rapidly changing relationship between school superintendents, secondary school principals, teachers, school boards, and the community. One need only refer to the prevalence of teacher strikes and sanctions to indicate how different is the scene today from what it was when I started the inquiry that led to my first report.

A last word to the interested citizen. I would ask him

to examine once again the data in Table 11 and what was said in Chapter 2 regarding the vast differences in the staff-student ratio from community to community and among different states. These variations are a reflection of the cost of providing education at the high school level. It is natural for a person to be concerned at first only with the excellence of his local public schools and the necessity in most cases of increasing the amount of money spent on them. But I suggest that one should also be concerned with the record of the entire state as illustrated by a number of the preceding tables in this text. To me it seems obvious that the great sums of money required for improving and expanding public education can only be found through new methods of financing. Finding such new methods will require strong leadership at both the state and local level by groups of distinguished citizens.

I hope in the next decade the American people will see to it that public education moves ahead toward a greater equality of opportunity. It is clear that a secondary school with a favorable staff-student ratio can provide effective guidance and rich programs suited to students with diverse interests and varying abilities. Once the significance of well-supported comprehensive high schools is fully grasped, I believe support will be forthcoming. Under such conditions these characteristic American institutions may well prove to be the most powerful instruments for the rapid improvement of the education of all the nation's youth.

Appendix

TABLE I. Types of school district organization by states, 1965–1966, showing number of schools responding to the questionnaire of December 1965 with the type of organization noted at the head of the column and the percentage

	4–4–4		5–3–4		6–2–4		6–3–3		6–6		8–4		Other	
	No.	%	No.	%	No.	%	No.	%	No.	%	No.	%	No.	%
Alabama	9	2.3	2	.5	22	5.5	197	49.6	118	29.7	20	5.0	29	7.
Alaska		.0	1	3.2	9	29.0	4	12.9	4	12.9	11	35.5	2	6.
Arizona	3	3.1	3	3.1	23	23.5	4	4.1	5	5.1	52	53.1	8	8.
Arkansas	1	.3	2	.7	20	6.8	58	19.7	192	65.1	14	4.7	8	2.
California	10	1.3	21	2.8	188	25.3	233	31.3	27	3.6	208	28.0	57	7.
Colorado	4	2.0	3	1.5	52	26.1	63	31.7	38	19.1	21	10.6	18	9.
Connecticut	5	3.5	10	7.0	28	19.6	34	23.8	31	21.7	23	16.1	12	8.
Delaware	1	3.0	1	3.0	7	21.2	10	30.3	11	33.3		.0	3	9.
D.C.		.0		.0		.0	21	84.0		.0	2	8.0	2	8.
Florida	4	1.2	32	9.7	20	6.1	190	57.6	47	14.2	9	2.7	28	8.
Georgia	15	3.9	24	6.2	39	10.1	33	8.5	16	4.1	123	31.8	137	35.
Hawaii		.0		.0	3	10.0	9	30.0	3	10.0	5	16.7	10	33.
Idaho	1	.8	3	2.3	59	45.7	23	17.8	14	10.9	22	17.1	7	5.
Illinois	13	1.7	56	7.3	172	22.3	52	6.8	13	1.7	410	53.2	54	7.0
Indiana		.0	14	2.8	128	25.7	73	14.7	171	34.3	75	15.1	37	7.
Iowa	1	.2	8	1.8	123	28.3	86	19.8	91	20.9	115	26.4	11	2.
Kansas	1	.3	4	1.0	28	7.2	44	11.3	13	3.4	280	72.2	18	4.6
Kentucky	3	1.3		.0	21	8.8	27	11.3	57	23.8	117	48.8	15	6.
Louisiana	3	.8	7	1.8	29	7.5	41	10.6	111	28.8	88	22.8	107	27.
Maine	7	5.3	11	8.3	28	21.1	21	15.8	17	12.8	38	28.6	11	8.
Maryland	1	.7	8	5.6	17	12.0	77	54.2	26	18.3	2	1.4	11	7.
Massachusetts	3	1.1	9	3.2	82	28.8	76	26.7	40	14.0	30	10.5	45	15.
Michigan	14	2.2	37	5.9	177	28.3	130	20.8	155	24.8	74	11.8	39	6.
Minnesota	1	.2	1	.2		.0	174	38.3	251	55.3	8	1.8	19	4.
Mississippi	2	.7	6	2.1	24	8.3	40	13.9	186	64.6	18	6.3	12	4.
Missouri	7	1.6	7	1.6	95	22.1	59	13.7	99	23.0	110	25.6	53	12.3

	4–4–4		5–3–4		6–2–4		6–3–3		6–6		8–4		Other	
	No.	%	No.	%	No.	%	No.	%	No.	%	No.	%	No.	%
Montana	1	.8	1	.8	14	10.6	12	9.1	10	7.6	90	68.2	4	3.0
Nebraska	1	.3	3	1.0	49	16.0	36	11.8	96	31.4	68	22.2	53	17.3
Nevada		.0		.0	1	2.9	9	25.7	7	20.0	14	40.0	4	11.4
New Hampshire	2	2.3	3	3.5	19	22.1	6	7.0	24	27.9	19	22.1	13	15.1
New Jersey	4	1.2	6	1.8	30	9.1	92	28.0	46	14.0	79	24.1	71	21.6
New Mexico	3	2.3	3	2.3	25	19.1	36	27.5	38	29.0	5	3.8	21	16.0
New York	53	5.9	35	3.9	114	12.7	272	30.2	289	32.1	43	4.8	94	10.4
North Carolina	59	10.8	2	.4	31	5.7	60	11.0	8	1.5	362	66.4	23	4.2
North Dakota	2	1.0	1	.5	29	14.7	13	6.6	42	21.3	91	46.2	19	9.6
Ohio	15	2.0	24	3.2	129	17.1	175	23.2	160	21.2	208	27.6	42	5.6
Oklahoma		.0	6	1.7	34	9.9	188	54.8	20	5.8	82	23.9	13	3.8
Oregon	4	2.0	4	2.0	18	9.0	40	20.0	11	5.5	108	54.0	15	7.5
Pennsylvania	2	.3	18	2.8	32	4.9	301	46.4	235	36.2	21	3.2	40	6.2
Rhode Island	1	2.9		.0	6	17.1	19	54.3	2	5.7	3	8.6	4	11.4
South Carolina	6	2.2	4	1.5	31	11.3	22	8.0	113	41.1	24	8.7	75	27.3
South Dakota		.0	1	.6	25	16.1	12	7.7	16	10.3	100	64.5	1	.6
Tennessee	7	2.2	3	.9	5	1.6	56	17.4	88	27.3	107	33.2	56	17.4
Texas	33	3.8	128	14.6	175	20.0	171	19.5	121	13.8	178	20.3	69	7.9
Utah		.0	2	2.9	3	4.3	41	58.6	15	21.4		.0	9	12.9
Vermont		.0	2	2.9	13	19.1	3	4.4	25	36.8	22	32.4	3	4.4
Virginia	1	.3	3	.9	42	12.8	30	9.2	8	2.4	15	4.6	228	69.7
Washington	2	.8	8	3.1	33	12.8	108	41.9	22	8.5	65	25.2	20	7.8
West Virginia		.0		.0	10	5.2	46	24.0	76	39.6	25	13.0	35	18.2
Wisconsin	2	.5	6	1.6	97	25.4	69	18.1	18	4.7	167	43.7	23	6.0
Wyoming		.0	1	1.6	24	38.7	7	11.3	11	17.7	15	24.2	4	6.5
Foreign		.0		.0	1	50.0		.0		.0	1	50.0		.0
TOTAL	307	2.0	535	3.4	2,388	15.3	3,646	23.3	3,254	20.8	3,794	24.3	1,704	10.9

TABLE II. Number and per cent of schools by enrollment category as of October 1, 1965, that responded to the questionnaire of December 1965

Enrollment

	0–499		500–749		750–999		1,000–1,999		2,000+	
	No.	%	No.	%	No.	%	No.	%	No.	%
Alabama	151	38.1	106	26.8	64	16.2	72	18.2	3	.8
Alaska	24	77.4	3	9.7	1	3.2	3	9.7		.0
Arizona	45	46.9	10	10.4	9	9.4	15	15.6	17	17.7
Arkansas	193	65.9	62	21.2	21	7.2	15	5.1	2	.7
California	129	17.7	62	8.5	53	7.3	265	36.5	218	30.0
Colorado	131	65.2	17	8.5	18	9.0	28	13.9	7	3.5
Connecticut	26	18.6	31	22.1	24	17.1	55	39.3	4	2.9
Delaware	6	17.1	9	25.7	7	20.0	13	37.1		.0
D.C.	3	13.0	4	17.4		.0	13	56.5	3	13.0
Florida	61	20.3	85	28.2	32	10.6	88	29.2	35	11.6
Georgia	95	26.4	94	26.1	79	21.9	85	23.6	7	1.9
Hawaii	2	6.9	5	17.2	4	13.8	10	34.5	8	27.6
Idaho	84	77.8	11	10.2	3	2.8	10	9.3		.0
Illinois	350	54.9	70	11.0	36	5.6	103	16.1	79	12.4
Indiana	199	42.7	118	25.3	58	12.4	65	13.9	26	5.6
Iowa	344	79.3	53	12.2	7	1.6	26	6.0	4	.9
Kansas	328	85.0	22	5.7	11	2.8	15	3.9	10	2.6
Kentucky	68	28.1	68	28.1	52	21.5	43	17.8	11	4.5
Louisiana	141	40.9	95	27.5	42	12.2	60	17.4	7	2.0
Maine	101	75.9	18	13.5	1	.8	13	9.8		.0
Maryland	27	18.8	23	16.0	27	18.8	46	31.9	21	14.6
Massachusetts	77	26.9	56	19.6	54	18.9	81	28.3	18	6.3
Michigan	216	38.3	135	23.9	59	10.5	107	19.0	47	8.3
Minnesota	298	66.4	63	14.0	31	6.9	46	10.2	11	2.4
Mississippi	73	29.7	74	30.1	45	18.3	50	20.3	4	1.6
Missouri	288	68.9	51	12.2	20	4.8	44	10.5	15	3.6

	0–499		500–749		750–999		1,000–1,999		2,000+	
	No.	%	No.	%	No.	%	No.	%	No.	%
Montana	111	84.1	9	6.8	5	3.8	6	4.5	1	.8
Nebraska	241	86.7	19	6.8	4	1.4	9	3.2	5	1.8
Nevada	23	69.7	4	12.1	1	3.0	4	12.1	1	3.0
New Hampshire	47	60.3	8	10.3	13	16.7	10	12.8		.0
New Jersey	14	5.2	33	12.3	60	22.4	137	51.1	24	9.0
New Mexico	59	63.4	12	12.9	5	5.4	13	14.0	4	4.3
New York	117	14.8	160	20.3	131	16.6	285	36.2	95	12.1
North Carolina	123	24.6	138	27.6	101	20.2	135	27.0	3	.6
North Dakota	176	89.8	10	5.1	6	3.1	4	2.0		.0
Ohio	277	37.5	182	24.7	84	11.4	159	21.5	36	4.9
Oklahoma	266	78.5	31	9.1	9	2.7	27	8.0	6	1.8
Oregon	121	59.9	34	16.8	10	5.0	27	13.4	10	5.0
Pennsylvania	101	15.9	168	26.4	130	20.4	190	29.9	47	7.4
Rhode Island	4	11.4	8	22.9	7	20.0	13	37.1	3	8.6
South Carolina	103	39.2	61	23.2	50	19.0	49	18.6		.0
South Dakota	141	90.4	9	5.8	4	2.6	1	.6	1	.6
Tennessee	111	35.5	86	27.5	37	11.8	69	22.0	10	3.2
Texas	593	67.2	95	10.8	44	5.0	101	11.4	50	5.7
Utah	41	57.7	8	11.3	4	5.6	12	16.9	6	8.5
Vermont	51	75.0	9	13.2	5	7.4	3	4.4		.0
Virginia	84	25.7	79	24.2	61	18.7	84	25.7	19	5.8
Washington	148	56.9	33	12.7	18	6.9	52	20.0	9	3.5
West Virginia	81	42.4	54	28.3	31	16.2	23	12.0	2	1.0
Wisconsin	196	51.3	79	20.7	35	9.2	58	15.2	14	3.7
Wyoming	48	77.4	6	9.7	4	6.5	4	6.5		.0
Foreign	4	8.9	16	35.6	7	15.6	13	28.9	5	11.1
TOTAL	6,763	45.5	2,706	18.2	1,624	11.0	2,863	19.3	908	6.1

TABLE IIIA. Number and per cent of medium-size comprehensive high school's offering advanced mathematics and calculus, by states

	No. of schools	Advanced mathematics offered		Calculus offered	
		No.	%	No.	%
Alabama	23	5	21.7	1	4.3
Alaska	3	1	33.3	1	33.3
Arizona	19	3	15.8	10	52.6
Arkansas	4	0	0.0	2	50.0
California	157	40	25.5	64	40.8
Colorado	23	5	21.7	8	34.8
Connecticut	34	5	14.7	26	76.5
Delaware	7	3	42.9	1	14.3
D.C.	5	2	40.0	2	40.0
Florida	49	12	24.5	19	38.8
Georgia	49	4	8.2	16	32.7
Hawaii	6	1	16.7	0	0.0
Idaho	5	0	0.0	3	60.0
Illinois	81	30	37.0	31	38.3
Indiana	55	13	23.6	27	49.1
Iowa	19	10	52.6	6	31.6
Kansas	19	8	42.1	9	47.4
Kentucky	27	2	7.4	9	33.3
Louisiana	22	3	13.6	5	22.7
Maine	12	0	0.0	9	75.0
Maryland	31	8	25.8	17	54.8
Massachusetts	72	12	16.7	46	63.9
Michigan	99	12	12.1	27	27.3
Minnesota	41	8	19.5	7	17.1
Mississippi	8	1	12.5	0	0.0
Missouri	37	11	29.7	10	27.0

	No. of schools	Advanced mathematics offered		Calculus offered	
		No.	%	No.	%
Montana	11	2	18.2	5	45.5
Nebraska	9	4	44.4	2	22.2
Nevada	5	2	40.0	3	60.0
New Hampshire	15	4	26.7	7	46.7
New Jersey	132	23	17.4	75	56.8
New Mexico	8	5	62.5	2	25.0
New York	145	60	41.4	93	64.1
North Carolina	66	9	13.6	15	22.7
North Dakota	3	0	0.0	1	33.3
Ohio	147	22	15.0	47	32.0
Oklahoma	14	2	14.3	5	35.7
Oregon	31	3	9.7	16	51.6
Pennsylvania	151	33	21.9	79	52.3
Rhode Island	9	3	33.3	5	55.6
South Carolina	29	4	13.8	10	34.5
South Dakota	3	0	0.0	0	0.0
Tennessee	42	4	9.5	9	21.4
Texas	69	27	39.1	7	10.1
Utah	10	3	30.0	3	30.0
Vermont	3	0	0.0	1	33.3
Virginia	63	10	15.9	15	23.8
Washington	55	23	41.8	28	50.9
West Virginia	31	3	9.7	8	25.8
Wisconsin	59	10	16.9	22	37.3
Wyoming	6	3	50.0	2	33.3
TOTAL	2,023	458	22.6	816	40.3

TABLE IIIB. Number and per cent of medium-size comprehensive high schools offering "new" sciences, by states

	No. of schools	"New" physics offered		"New" biology offered		"New" chemistry offered	
		No.	%	No.	%	No.	%
Alabama	23	8	34.8	10	43.5	7	30.4
Alaska	3	3	100.0	3	100.0	2	66.7
Arizona	19	5	26.3	12	63.2	8	42.1
Arkansas	4	0	0.0	1	25.0	0	0.0
California	157	103	65.6	136	86.6	108	68.8
Colorado	23	15	65.2	22	95.7	16	69.6
Connecticut	34	20	58.8	18	52.9	13	38.2
Delaware	7	4	57.1	6	85.7	5	71.4
D.C.	5	2	40.0	4	80.0	1	20.0
Florida	49	40	81.6	44	89.8	32	65.3
Georgia	49	15	30.6	35	71.4	17	34.7
Hawaii	6	4	66.7	6	100.0	5	83.3
Idaho	5	1	20.0	3	60.0	2	40.0
Illinois	81	45	55.6	59	72.8	45	55.6
Indiana	55	18	32.7	29	52.7	18	32.7
Iowa	19	11	57.9	14	73.7	10	52.6
Kansas	19	13	68.4	14	73.7	14	73.7
Kentucky	27	7	25.9	12	44.4	5	18.5
Louisiana	22	8	36.4	9	40.9	4	18.2
Maine	12	8	66.7	9	75.0	4	33.3
Maryland	31	22	71.0	26	83.9	14	45.2
Massachusetts	72	50	69.4	54	75.0	48	66.7
Michigan	99	42	42.4	58	58.6	39	39.4
Minnesota	41	25	61.0	27	65.9	25	61.0
Mississippi	8	1	12.5	2	25.0	3	37.5
Missouri	37	14	37.8	21	56.8	12	32.4

	No. of schools	"New" physics offered		"New" biology offered		"New" chemistry offered	
		No.	%	No.	%	No.	%
Montana	11	5	45.5	8	72.7	5	45.5
Nebraska	9	5	55.6	5	55.6	5	55.6
Nevada	5	1	20.0	4	80.0	3	60.0
New Hampshire	15	10	66.7	10	66.7	9	60.0
New Jersey	132	87	65.9	82	62.1	69	52.3
New Mexico	8	4	50.0	6	75.0	2	25.0
New York	145	51	35.2	69	47.6	58	40.0
North Carolina	66	21	31.8	40	60.6	17	25.8
North Dakota	3	0	0.0	3	100.0	1	33.3
Ohio	147	55	37.4	75	51.0	60	40.8
Oklahoma	14	9	64.3	8	57.1	7	50.0
Oregon	31	26	83.9	27	87.1	25	80.6
Pennsylvania	151	70	46.4	97	64.2	74	49.0
Rhode Island	9	4	44.4	6	66.7	5	55.6
South Carolina	29	8	27.6	15	51.7	9	31.0
South Dakota	3	2	66.7	2	66.7	2	66.7
Tennessee	42	6	14.3	14	33.3	9	21.4
Texas	69	28	40.6	46	66.7	26	37.7
Utah	10	3	30.0	8	80.0	5	50.0
Vermont	3	2	66.7	3	100.0	0	0.0
Virginia	63	22	34.9	40	63.5	20	31.7
Washington	55	47	85.5	51	92.7	40	72.7
West Virginia	31	12	38.7	11	35.5	15	48.4
Wisconsin	59	36	61.0	45	76.3	36	61.0
Wyoming	6	3	50.0	3	50.0	3	50.0
TOTAL	2,023	1,001	49.5	1,312	64.9	962	47.6

TABLE IV. Number of medium-size comprehensive high schools with counselor-student ratio of 1:350 or better, English teacher load 120 or less, offering four years of a foreign language, four-year mathematics program, calculus, "new" physics, chemistry, or biology, vocational instruction, music and art, and having 7,500 or more books in the library. Reported by state and enrollment categories

| | Enrollment category | | | |
	750–999	1,000–1,499	1,500–1,999	TOTAL
California	1	2		3
Connecticut			1	1
Georgia			1	1
Illinois		2	3	5
Indiana	2			2
Kansas	1			1
Maine		1		1
Massachusetts	3	5	1	9
Nevada			1	1
New Hampshire		1		1
New Jersey	7	11	3	21
New York	12	17	5	34
Ohio			3	3
Oregon	1			1
Pennsylvania	4		2	6
Texas		1		1
Washington		1		1
Wisconsin	1			1
TOTAL	32	41	20	93

TABLE V.   Number of volumes in the libraries of medium-size comprehensive high schools by categories and size of schools

Size measured by enrollment	Number of schools	0–7,499 volumes		7,500–9,999 volumes		10,000–14,999 volumes		15,000+ volumes	
		No.	%	No.	%	No.	%	No.	%
750–999	678	400	59.0	157	23.2	111	16.4	10	1.5
1,000–1,499	836	328	39.2	254	30.4	217	26.0	37	4.4
1,500–1,999	501	80	16.0	134	26.7	219	43.7	68	13.6
TOTAL	2,015	808	40.1	545	27.0	547	27.1	115	5.7

BLE VI.   Number and per cent of medium-size comprehensive high ools by enrollment categories having one or more assistant principals

measured by rollment	Number of schools	No ass't. reported		One ass't.		Two ass't.		Three ass't.		Four ass't.		Five ass't.		Six or more ass't.	
		No.	%	No.	%	No.	%	No.	%	No.	%	No.	%	No.	%
50–999	681	136	19.9	473	69.4	67	9.8	5	.9	0	.0	0	.0	0	.0
00–1,499	841	44	5.2	550	65.4	213	25.3	29	3.4	4	.4	0	.0	1	.1
00–1,999	502	8	1.5	216	43.0	189	37.6	80	15.9	8	1.6	1	.1	0	.0
TOTAL	2,024	188	9.3	1,239	61.2	469	23.2	114	5.6	12	.6	1	–	1	–

TABLE VII. Number and per cent of medium-size comprehensive secondary schools offering four years of a modern foreign language

	No. reporting	4 yrs. lang.	Per cent
Ala.	23	1	4.3
Alas.	3	3	100.0
Ariz.	19	12	63.1
Ark.	4	2	50.0
Cal.	157	127	80.9
Colo.	23	18	78.3
Conn.	34	31	.91.2
Del.	7	7	100.0
D.C.	5	4	80.0
Fla.	49	25	51.0
Ga.	49	15	30.6
Hawa.	6	0	0
Ida.	5	1	20.0
Ill.	81	57	70.3
Ind.	55	31	56.3
Iowa	19	15	78.9
Kans.	19	8	42.1
Ky.	27	7	25.9
La.	22	6	26.8
Me.	12	9	75.0
Md.	31	29	93.5
Mass.	72	61	84.7
Mich.	99	38	39.3
Minn.	41	24	58.5
Miss.	8	2	25.0

	No. reporting	4 yrs. lang.	Per cent
Mo.	36	19	52.8
Mont.	11	6	54.5
Neb.	9	3	33.3
Nev.	5	3	60.0
N.H.	15	14	93.3
N.J.	133	124	92.4
N.M.	8	2	25.0
N.Y.	144	124	86.0
N.C.	64	25	39.0
N.D.	3	1	33.3
Ohio	147	92	62.6
Okla.	14	5	35.7
Ore.	31	24	77.5
Penna.	151	128	84.7
R.I.	9	8	88.8
S.C.	28	10	35.7
S.D.	3	2	66.6
Tenn.	42	7	16.6
Tex.	69	25	36.2
Utah	10	4	40.0
Vt.	3	3	100.0
Va.	63	33	52.3
Wash.	55	31	56.4
W. Va.	31	12	38.7
Wisc.	59	48	81.3
Wyo.	6	4	66.6
TOTAL	2,019	1,290	63.9

TABLE VIII.   Further data on correlation

[The correlation between staff-student ratio and certain offerings treated below is particularly well brought out by classifying the reporting schools into three groups as follows: schools in which 25–39 per cent of the 1965 graduates proceeded with further education, 40–59 per cent and 60–74 per cent. In the tables shown below it will be noted that the numbers in the first group are small and in the second and third groups relatively large; in the second and third groups the correlation is most striking.]

A. Calculus offered

Staff-student ratio	Number of schools reporting	25–39 per cent 1965 graduates continued in post–H.S. education		40–59 per cent 1965 graduates continued in post–H.S. education		60–74 per cent 1965 graduates continued in post–H.S. education		Total 25–74 per cent 1965 graduates continued in post–H.S. education	
		No.	%	No.	%	No.	%	No.	%
17.4 or less	357	16	4.5	92	25.7	102	28.5	210	58.7
17.5–20.4	680	28	4.1	129	18.9	96	14.1	253	37.1
20.5–23.4	664	31	4.7	109	16.4	84	12.7	224	33.7
23.5–26.4	258	14	5.6	21	8.1	28	10.9	63	24.6
26.5 or more	60	4	6.7	6	10.0	8	13.3	18	30.0
TOTAL	2,019	93	4.6	357	17.6	318	15.7	768	38.0

B. Four years of any one modern foreign language offered

Staff-student ratio	Number of schools reporting	25–39 per cent 1965 graduates continuing in post–H.S. education		40–59 per cent 1965 graduates continuing in post–H.S. education		60–74 per cent 1965 graduates continuing in post–H.S. education		Total 25–74 per cent 1965 graduates continuing in post–H.S. education	
		No.	%	No.	%	No.	%	No.	%
17.4 or less	357	19	5.3	151	42.5	142	40.0	312	87.4
17.5–20.4	680	65	9.6	234	34.4	171	25.1	470	69.1
20.5–23.4	664	61	9.2	181	27.2	121	18.2	363	54.7
23.5–26.4	258	15	5.8	49	19.0	53	20.5	117	45.3
26.5 or more	60	3	5.0	14	23.3	11	18.2	28	46.6
TOTAL	2,019	163	8.0	629	31.1	498	24.6	1,290	63.8

C. Advanced placement program offered

Staff-student ratio	Number of schools reporting	25–39 per cent 1965 graduates continued in post–H.S. education		40–59 per cent 1965 graduates continued in post–H.S. education		60–74 per cent 1965 graduates continued in post–H.S. education		Total 25–74 per cent 1965 graduates continued in post–H.S. education	
		No.	%	No.	%	No.	%	No.	%
17.4 or less	357	5	1.4	61	17.0	89	24.9	155	43.4
17.5–20.4	680	26	3.8	92	13.5	86	12.6	204	30.0
20.5–23.4	664	16	2.4	92	13.8	94	14.1	202	30.4
23.5–26.4	258	11	4.2	19	7.3	17	6.6	47	18.2
26.5 or more	60	2	3.3	2	3.3	6	10.0	10	16.6
TOTAL	2,019	60	2.9	266	13.2	292	14.5	618	30.6

D. Schedule permits students to take five academic subjects, physical education, and art or music in any one year

Staff-student ratio	Number of schools reporting	25–39 per cent 1965 graduates continued in post–H.S. education		40–59 per cent 1965 graduates continued in post–H.S. education		60–74 per cent 1965 graduates continued in post–H.S. education		Total 25–74 per cent 1965 graduates continued in post–H.S. education	
		No.	%	No.	%	No.	%	No.	%
17.4 or less	357	25	7.0	149	41.7	131	36.7	305	85.4
17.5–20.4	680	67	9.8	255	37.5	165	24.2	487	71.6
20.5–23.4	664	82	12.3	212	31.9	126	19.0	420	63.2
23.5–26.4	258	27	10.4	74	28.6	62	24.0	163	63.1
26.5 or more	60	7	11.6	17	28.3	14	23.3	38	63.3
TOTAL	2,019	208	10.3	707	35.0	498	24.6	1,413	70.0

E. English teacher load, 120 or less

Staff-student ratio	Number of schools reporting	25–39 per cent 1965 graduates continued in post–H.S. education		40–59 per cent 1965 graduates continued in post–H.S. education		60–74 per cent 1965 graduates continued in post–H.S. education		Total 25–74 per cent 1965 graduates continued in post–H.S. education	
		No.	%	No.	%	No.	%	No.	%
17.4 or less	357	8	2.2	94	26.3	101	28.3	203	56.8
17.5–20.4	680	23	3.3	95	13.9	62	9.1	180	26.4
20.5–23.4	664	16	2.4	34	5.1	28	4.2	78	11.7
23.5–26.4	258	4	1.5	14	5.4	8	3.1	26	10.0
26.5 or more	60	3	5.0	3	5.0	1	1.6	7	11.6
TOTAL	2,019	54	2.6	240	11.8	200	9.9	494	24.4